I was the youngest of 10 children, raised by my parents in Cockfield, Bury St Edmunds. I was educated at the local voluntary school in our village.

I worked on a local farm, also with a local butcher, both lovely families from the village, before I was called up for duty in the Army.

After the war, I was offered a heavy goods driving role; sadly being around six stone, this was all too much for me, but I had a very patient and understanding employer. With his help and that of my friends and family, I came through to better health and strength, enabling me to stay in the driving profession for my working days.

I was a deacon at our local Cockfield Congregational Chapel, also a lay preacher for many years. I now live in town with my wife, still tending our small pretty garden and am looked after by my daughter and son-in-law.

UNBELIEVABLE BUT TRUE—STORY OF CAPTIVITY

Grace

Sidney Lockwood

Unbelievable But
True–Story Of Captivity

Best Wishes

Sidney R Lockwood

MAY 2006

Vanguard Press

VANGUARD PAPERBACK

A CIP catalogue record for this title is available from the British Library

ISBN 1 84386 242 5

Vanguard Press is an imprint of
Pegasus Elliot MacKenzie Publishers Ltd.
www.pegasuspublishers.com

First Published in 2006

Vanguard Press
Sheraton House Castle Park
Cambridge England

Printed & Bound in Great Britain

Dedication

I dedicate this book to my daughter Barbara and son-in-law Gerry, in great appreciation for all they have done for me.

Also to my dear wife Joyce, for her love and patience over the years.

Sidney

Foreword

One evening after supper I began to read the manuscript of Sidney Lockwood's remarkable story of captivity by the Japanese during World War Two. It was New Year and the Honours list had just been announced. Some newspapers were indignant that a well-known entertainer had not been granted one of the higher honours whilst a popular singer had been knighted. In the light of Sidney's book it all seemed trivial. True, both artists were professionals in their field and had kept their names well before the public for many a year. Sidney, along with so many of his comrades belonged to the forgotten generation. The men and women who were proud to serve their King and country during the Second World War and who suffered dreadfully as a result.

During the day I phoned one of these old survivors and without my prompting he made reference to the Honours list. 'We have been forgotten' he said, 'who cares or even knows what we had to endure during those terrible years.' The 'forgetting' began almost as soon as Sidney Lockwood arrived back in the United Kingdom following his release. He had been told that an Army car would be on hand to meet him at Bury St Edmunds Railway Station where he arrived during the early hours of the morning. There was no car, just two Military Policemen who didn't expect him but managed to get him a shared taxi back to his home village. For that he had to pay two pounds from his own pocket. That was a considerable sum in those days. It was this chapter that brought tears to my eyes.

During the course of the book he describes the most terrible deprivations he and his companions suffered. Although I was appalled at the descriptions of man's inhumanity to man it was the homecoming that moved me more than anything else. The picture of a man scarred in mind and body making his lonely way home in the knowledge that both his mother and father had died during his absence was heart rending. I well remember how long and hard many of us had to fight to get the British Government to make a simple one off payment to the elderly survivors of the Japanese Camps. Eventually they each received a small sum some fifty years after release. It wasn't compensation, for nothing could possibly compensate for what they experienced. The vast majority did not want compensation. They deserved a simple acknowledgement that as young men they had given everything so that we might enjoy freedom today. The payment was a token.

Like so many ex-prisoners of the Japanese Sidney buried the experience deep within himself and attempted to resume normal life. Gradually, over the years, thanks to the companionship of those in the Far Eastern Prisoners of War Association and especially to his loving and understanding daughter Barbara, he was able to articulate the past and the result is this truly outstanding book. Sidney has provided a well written first hand account of captivity and although the sufferings are truly appalling there is not a trace of bitterness in his writing. He makes no bones about the fact that he is a Christian but at no point does he wear his religion on his sleeve. Sidney reminds us of the evils of warfare and of the fact that deep within all of us, regardless of creed or culture, there is an element of cruelty and inhumanity. And yet, in the midst of such deprivation the human spirit is given a chance to shine and shine it does.

World War Two and the Japanese camps are a long way behind us now thank God but atrocities continue throughout the world. This book ought to be put into the hands of every sixth former in the United Kingdom lest we forget. It also ought to be read by entertainers, civil servants and all who feel hard done by. Sidney speaks of true courage and loyalty. There will be many readers of this book who will give him and his companions true honour and respect.

Terry Waite CBE 2006

CONTENTS

INTRODUCTION

A true story of torture and survival under the Imperial Japanese Army during the Second World War

This personal story is told by my father, Sidney Richard Lockwood, born on 14th December 1919 to Sarah and Herbert Lockwood of Cockfield, Bury St Edmunds in Suffolk. Being the youngest of ten children, he tells of his childhood, his personal experiences and those as a young man, called upon to do his duty to King and Country.

Sidney joined up on 10th March 1940 and was eventually drafted into the 2nd Cambridgeshire Regiment. Here is a copy of their much coveted army crest.

REGIMENTAL CREST 2ND CAMBRIDGESHIRES

Sidney was sent off to an unknown destination in October 1941. He was captured by the Japanese on the 15th February 1942 and was held captive for three and a half arduous years.

Today he bears no hatred to his Japanese captors, saying he

was luckier than some. Throughout all of the squalid days of captivity, through sickness, brutality and degradation in those camps of hell, where many thousands of men died; he maintained his faith in God above.

It took him years to be able to tell us of his captivity and to this day he still speaks with real passion and deep feeling towards his comrades, both those deceased and living. Those friends fortunate enough to have survived the same ordeal and still remarkably are around today, he counts amongst his dearest and truest friends. There is never a day that goes by but what he refers to one or the other of them, or that he fondly recalls some memory of times past.

As his daughter, I have become extremely interested in his army days and his life story over the years. I have read many books written by fellow POWs and their accounts have been moving to read. This has driven my desire, so much so, that I felt compelled to help my dear dad in whatever way I could, to encourage him to express his feelings in writing.

For almost 50 years he could scarcely speak of his own terrible experiences. So deeply buried within him were his memories about those horrific years in captivity that tears would freely flow, making it difficult, near impossible for him to tell me his story. But when he did, I realised it was something that just simply had to be shared.

You can read as many stories as you like, watch as many films as you like too, but that can only leave you imagining the reality and extent of what actually went on. Hearing these accounts first hand, recording onto tape his words, seeing and feeling the raw emotion even sixty years on, can only in part relay the depth of gratitude that should be offered to these men and those alike, that have served in the forces, throughout generations and down through the years. All for our liberty and freedom, which sadly all too often we abuse.

We must not take for granted their heroic efforts, that wasn't what their sacrifice was all about, I'm sure. They endured the war for us, their offspring and future generation. Without question an act of true courage and bravery on behalf of each and every man, deeds and actions that should never be underestimated, taken for granted or above all be forgotten and lost in the mists of time.

Latterly, well into his own retirement years, Dad joined a local reunion club in his home town and gradually became able to express his thoughts and recollections of those terrible years of captivity in the jungles of Thailand, under the Imperial Japanese Army. I recall vividly the many marches that he took part in. Some in Ely and one in particular will always spring back to my mind, when the ex-POWs were marching down Churchgate Street in Bury St Edmunds. The one way street having been closed to allow their procession to march down towards our local cathedral.

Apart from their sombre faces bravely facing forward, they marched like young soldiers, each and every one concentrating on his own footsteps, and it was those footsteps that I recall so vividly. Not a sound emerged from anywhere, the silent crowd pressing to see them, but there was just this echo, quite a loud echo in that narrow street, of weary older men's footsteps, all proudly making a bold statement.

Those same footsteps that must have scarred the earth around the tropical jungle that once was their "home" for so many long years, whilst building that notorious and unforgettable railway.

Here they were though, many still safe and sound, quiet and dignified, no doubt mournful in their own thoughts and feelings but proudly wearing their regimental ties, with their medals shone to perfection. Not a word was spoken. It didn't have to be. It wasn't necessary, as the silence said it all. Just the echo of those footsteps, coming at you from the distance, getting louder as they pasted immediately by you and then trailing away off into the next street, all in a very hushed silence as they neared the cathedral for their Service of Remembrance.

<u>DAD IN HIS MID 70s DRESSED READY FOR ONE OF HIS PARADES AND PROUDLY WEARING HIS REGIMENTAL UNIFORM</u>

REGIMENTAL MARCH

People openly have said they do not believe some of the stories of Dad's accounts and so together we have spent many hours piecing together this unbelievable but true story. Tapes have been recorded and notes have been written and typed. Together we have travelled back through those years, through those jungle cuttings, through the ill treatment and starvation and have put together his remarkable personal journey.

We have not recorded how the war happened or even why. Many great historians over the decades have already penned us such information and in much more detail than we are even obliged to know or gifted to entertain writing about. We have simply compiled in our own style, his accounts of what he personally witnessed and what Dad endured for the many years he was held prisoner by another country and its fearful army of men.

Dad says it was not all doom and gloom as POWs would always make the best of a very bad situation; men always were willing to help each other out with a smile or a joke to try to ease the heartache. Even now having typed his words, he seldom if ever, appeared angry at what happened to him. What a gift to be able to forgive so much, handed out for so long. If only I could claim that I had the same attribute and feelings given his circumstances.

I'm truly humbled and proud of my father's attitude towards the Japanese people who inflicted all of this upon him.

Since listening intently to his stories I feel I have been there with him in that jungle and it has always been my ambition to go to Singapore to see for myself where he and many like him were. One day I might be able to go to the Far East and see all the places we have talked about and I'm sure my emotions will be moved in a way such as he displays today, seeing the parts of the railway that still fortunately exist and recall all the countless numbers of lives that were needlessly lost.

I am unable to liken his words and experiences of such sheer hard labour to anything whatsoever in my life. Suffice to say that recently I removed a line of conifer trees from my garden. For those of you that have undertaken this task you will know when I say it is extremely hard work indeed, especially when undertaken by hand. Certainly a task you wouldn't choose to perform during a tropical storm or an intense heat wave, but they did. Those conifer roots were nowhere as penetrable and stubborn as those of bamboo. I could stop for a glass of cold fizzy drink or water from the tap when I wanted to, something they couldn't do. I could sit down to rest and to get a second wind so to speak, something they dare not do. I could revive my flagging energy by resting properly at the end of the day when the job was completed, something they had no say over. I didn't have to do that same back-breaking job the next day or the next week or indeed the next month or the next year... they had no choice whatsoever. They were brutally forced on and on and on, for what turned out to be years. It truly must have felt like an eternity to them all. I will never complain at facing such a menial task again, compared to them moving miles and miles of forest after forest, and all under such wicked circumstances.

I consider myself extremely lucky indeed to have my Dad with me today, and thank him for his guidance and for his life time devotion to my dear mum, who has had to rely very heavily upon him, as she needs his constant support through ailing health.

Dad showed through those arduous and torturous years as a prisoner of war that he is a long suffering, forgiving and a very patient and loving man. Qualities together with his Christian beliefs that he still clearly shows and demonstrates to us all today. I know that I owe him, his many comrades and many more that perished, a debt that I will never be able to repay. I do feel so very privileged to have such a father, my dear dad and my best friend.

Barbara Summons
(Daughter)

CHAPTER ONE

ABOUT TO SERVE MY KING

Little did I think when I was so young that I would end up as a prisoner of war. I was the youngest of ten children and my father, Herbert, was a farm labourer who specialised in poultry and geese in particular, being a stock man for a local farmer in Cockfield.

A MUCH PRIZED AND RARE PHOTOGRAPH OF ALL THE LOCKWOOD FAMILY

Our local shop keeper Mr White relayed a story to me about my father, Herbert, and how he used to watch him go past his village store, walking with some 1000 geese that had arrived by cattle trucks at our railway station. He would then be in charge of driving the geese (or shacking them, as it was known) on past our largest village green and into Green Farm where he worked. He was helped with this task by his older sons and other men from the village. (I was yet to arrive on the scene). The geese used to be kept there in sheds until father had sorted them out and then the geese were let loose on the green to graze.

What a sight that must have been and the noise from the gaggling must have been deafening. Today we would be hustling them off for fear of them stripping the village green bare.

My mother was a very good cook indeed but I guess you'd expect me to say that, she was also very strict with us children. Everything was either home reared, home grown or home baked and if it was to be an egg shared between two children, then that is what it was and no squabbling allowed either.

I recall her lovely Yorkshire puddings. She would make one large one and cut it into squares. Don't forget that would have to go between the twelve of us in total. Mainly we put brown sugar and vinegar on it, which was considered a real tasty treat.

Mother made apple pies that were to die for. We were lucky we had a large Doctor Harvey apple tree in the garden and that helped enormously with her meagre budget in those days. Mother also prepared a tasty egg custard. I don't recall much about breakfast I think it must have been porridge but we usually ate our main meal in the evenings together.

I do recall mother taking father his hot dinner across the meadows to him at work on a daily basis, complete with me and sister Violet in tow. It was taken on a big special double plate, which had a hot water layer beneath, with a plug in it to keep the food hot. He was mighty grateful for her efforts I know that, because at the time he was digging out a river, cleaning it up, working about two miles across from our home, and my father unfortunately by this time was crippled up with arthritis. Seeing his family complete with hot dinner, trudging towards him must have been a warming sight for father and so our life went happily on, until the onset of war.

As a young man embarking out into employment in the big wide world, I worked for a very well known local farmer, Mr

Hodge. I cut many a hedge around his property but my main recollections of those early days, is that of working with the farm horses. Captain, Dobbin, Dolly and Smiler were their names, and faithful and reliable creatures they were to work with too.

These animals were used by the horse men and helped us to plough the fields, reap in the harvest and many more arduous tasks that we had no mechanical implements for at the time. My task with them was to go stone picking and carting these stones back to the farm area, where the stones would be used in the mixing of cement and then used for building and setting up foundations. Lime spreading and muck carting are just to name but another two jobs we used these adorable creatures for.

ANOTHER VALUED PHOTOGRAPH OF ME WORKING WITH SOME OF THOSE HORSES

SOME OF THE GOLDING FAMILY FROM COCKFIELD

Later on I was privileged to work for the Golding family also from Cockfield. Here is where I learnt what was to be my main occupation after the war, that of a driver. The Goldings helped me through that chapter in my life and mighty pleased I am for their support. I ended up helping in their butchery shop The Shambles in Bury St Edmunds and became a meat delivery van driver. Needless to say Mrs Golding provided us boys with a marvellous cooked breakfast, with as much meat as you could manage, which was a real godsend.

CAR I PASSED MY TEST IN (PICTURED WITH WORKING COLLEAGUE WILF GOODCHILD

I received my call-up papers on March 10th 1940 and went off on the local train from my home village of Cockfield to Bury St Edmunds to join the queue at Gibraltar Barracks. It was snowing heavily, a really terrible day. We were standing there three or four deep, hundreds of us young men, and that is where I caught up with Charlie Marsh and one or two more that I knew and stood chatting with them, watching the earlier recruits doing a bayonet charge on the parade ground. We said we would never be able to do that, but within a few days we were practising that same bayonet charge and being watched by yet more new recruits, waiting to join up as we had done a few days earlier.

WHEN I JOINED UP IN 1940

We had six months at Gibraltar Barracks in training and originally I was placed in the Suffolk Regiment but later transferred to the 2nd Cambridgeshires to help make them up to strength and posted to Swan Lodge, Holt in Norfolk.

During this time I was to become engaged to Joyce, my now dear wife of some 58 years. It was her picture and memories of her, along with those of my dear family that carried me through the darkest of days that later were to follow.

Our regiment had several months at Holt. It was around there that I won a cross-country race, or should I say I came in third, to be honest, winning my first medal. Little did I realise I was about to have three more medals bestowed upon me in later years. The battalion moved to Sheringham seaside town, and there we used to go to a well-known little café. It used to be a real tasty treat to go in there on a Friday night for egg and chips, about 1s. 9d as I recall. That wouldn't be every week, mind you, just when we could really afford it. What later transpired as we were told by our commanding officers back at Holt was that someone who worked there was a Nazi spy. The waters around Sheringham are quite deep even towards the coastline, and German submarines used to navigate close to the mainland, where upon our café spy, from his bedroom window, used to signal all the news he had managed to over hear from us soldiers as we partook of his delightful suppers.

We were moved onto Harply in King's Lynn, being billeted in a local Sunday School. It was there that my good friend Percy Legge (Leggy) was implicated in killing a noisy cockerel which was hidden up high on the roof, as later it was to be cooked and eaten. He was never found out and no one let on who it was, although the local people soon noticed the noisy cockerel's absence, so you see even in these early days loyalties to each other were beginning to form.

Later we were transferred to Dumfries in Scotland and we were to have some lovely times up there training in the hills. Victor Mortlock, a very dear friend indeed, and myself were chosen to go to the chapel services in Motherwell and we enjoyed them very much. I recall a favourite haunt of ours was the local cake shop where you could buy six tasty fairy cakes for 12p. Friday was pay day so guess where our first port of call was! One other treat whilst in Dumfries was that of the use of the local showers. We were allowed 17 minutes exactly to carry out the necessary bathing requirements. We made the most of those 17 minutes I can tell you.

Later it was on to Crewe and we carried on with our training in and around the Cheshire/Welsh borders. It was during 1941 that I received a letter from home informing me that my older brother Jack had been killed in service out in Belgium. We had three embarkation leaves in total from Crewe, allowing us to go home for a week at a time. It was on the last of those three visits that little did I realise I was to say goodbye to my dear mother and father for the final time. This was October 1941 and I can recall my father's words to me as we kissed goodbye. He said, "Boy, never lose sight of Jesus." Am I glad to be able to recall his words so vividly today and even happier that I chose to follow in his footsteps.

My older brother Jack had already sadly been killed in the war and it was May time when brothers Tom and Peg (Edgar) were to be called to join up.

Joyce came to see me off at the station on the final visit and with the help of David Golding, a really lovely man and sincere friend whom I deeply miss even now, both waved me off at the station.

On return to Crewe we packed everything up and cleared camp, including most of our kit and sports gear. All the hardware, grey painted equipment for the theatre of war, Bren guns, and carriers, all of this was sent via Crewe railway station en route to the docks, where the dockers handled all of that cargo for our section.

This equipment was to go out on a separate boat to that of the men folk. We merely took our own personal kit then made for Gourock on the Clyde in Scotland. Here I was to join my first ship the "Sobieski". It was the first ship I had ever seen in my life. What a sight to behold. It was a Polish cattle boat and I boarded this now troop carrier mid October 1941. Come to that I had never been out on the ocean before or sailed the high seas, so I was in for the adventure of a lifetime. Some adventure this turned out to be in later years. It ended up feeling like a lifetime too, but for now, many thousands of troops and scores of boats or I should say ships, were all about to set sail for unknown destinations. We could be going anywhere in the world, or so it felt at the time. There was a buzz in the air but in truth we were all novices and not best prepared for what was to come. What skills were lacking now were no doubt going to be drilled or instilled into us one way or the other and pretty quickly too!

THE SOBIESKI

These were indeed unusual times; mixing and working with men who yesterday were strangers, and now we were shoulder to shoulder. Potentially men at war, comrades in arms. All sent to protect our homeland and to help other people's threatened countries, supporting those who needed our help. I had not envisaged this happening to me whilst helping Dad back on his allotment in Cockfield.

We loaded up with all our kit and arms, and then set sail. A strange feeling leaving dear old England behind in our wake, but all too soon we ground to a halt and lay off the coast of Ireland for three days allowing for the rest of the ships to assemble in our convoy. Now it was beginning to sink in that we were actually off to war, to serve our King and Country. There were 22 ships in our convoy. All assembling in formation, an experience to see and witness and to be in amongst, I can tell you. So eventually off we sailed "destination unknown" via

Greenland and on down to Halifax, Nova Scotia.

Whilst en route sailing on the "Sobieski", Bren gun nests were obviously set up on deck and I along with some others were on watch, taking our turn on the outward journey. When to our utter surprise, overhead and from nowhere, roared this almighty big plane. Luckily enough for him we were not quick enough to take aim. Good job we didn't, as it was an American aircraft. So it wasn't a case of holding fire, he was luckily out of range due to the sheer surprise of the aircraft appearing overhead so quickly, and all before we could have a chance to down him, and down him we would have too. Due to the jittery nature and happenings of war at the time anything could have taken place, but this pilot luckily escaped.

I recall the captain of this vessel. He was a short rather rotund, man, always wearing a hat and with one huge long black beard. After the war it came to my ears that this captain had been sailing en route to and from Japan, plus many other ports, I'm sure, and he had stayed away from home and remained on the high seas for four years in total.

One soldier thought he could get the better of the "Sobieski" and decided he would unlawfully climb up the outside of the deck areas, from the bottom of the ship to the top. But unfortunately and to his cost he chose to do this daring climb during heavy seas. The sea got the better of him to say the least. He was using some sort of ladder system that was rigged up and he was over three parts of the way to the top when the waves pounded the vessel, tossing us about like a cork and down he came. His daredevil escapade broke his back and he was flown off to a nearby hospital.

We arrived November 5th 1941 and I was fortunate enough by this time to have been made up to a lance corporal and "in charge" so to speak, and so I fortunately helped with the unloading of the 6000 personal kit bags, along with that of the officers, all of which had to be transported by road across to the other docks in Halifax. So I was very, very lucky and privileged to get to see some of Canada for myself as we travelled across to the other dockland. It was there we transferred from the "Sobieski" to the "Mount Vernon". This ship was absolutely enormous. The "Sobieski" paled into her shadows by way of size. I could hardly believe my own eyes at the sight and size of this magnificent ship; it was awesome. After some time and working all through the night handling the goods and stores which we could manhandle, all the soldiers safely transferred to their new ship, “The Mount Vernon”.

THE MOUNT VERNON

(Shown, as she was originally named, as the “Washington”)

Whilst on board the “Mount Vernon” some deaths did occur and these men were buried at sea in lead coffins. I watched such a service taking place. This ship was from the United States of America and was previously named the “SS Washington”.

On about the 11th November 1941 we set sail again down the east coast of America past Trinidad and there we stood off shore for refuelling and restocking of food. No shore leave was allowed but there was plenty to watch going on at this time and I recall the Americans taking the mickey out of us. Because they knew being British we were used to going short of food in England and they went short of nothing, saying, "You ain’t seen nothing yet. You’ll soon have more food than you can all eat."

Those words were to echo in our ears months later and even

before that, about a fortnight into our voyage the brigadier in charge of our convoy said our meals were to be drastically cut, in preparation for what awaited us presumably; otherwise they wouldn't be able to do anything with us. But for all that the food was very good.

We had to stand up to take our meals in long mess rooms with tables, food being served up on prepared trays. The way it worked was every man picked up a tray which was already laden with anything and everything you could wish for. Meat, vegetables, fruit and more. If you couldn't eat it all, someone was always near by whose appetite was still ravenous so with hindsight it was right to cut us back when they did in preparation for the days of starvation that unknowingly were to follow.

Whilst on board ship, in the evenings we were allowed to go down below decks to have a game of bingo. We played with real money. One bloke who ran the bingo made enough money to send back to England to buy his wife a brand new car. That was in the days when a Ford model car could be purchased for £100.

There were 6000 or more troops on board and around 300 or more of us would attend Sunday Service lead by our padre. It wasn't compulsory to go to Sunday Service but despite the number in proportion I have to say the singing was jolly good, resounding loudly off the steel sides of our ship.

Our sleeping quarters were that of two and three tier bunks. We didn't have to keep watch or anything like that at the time because this was all carried out by the Americans running the vessel.

Our officers ensured we carried out our daily drill and physical training with route marches around the deck itself to keep us in peak condition for what was to follow. We attended lectures about warfare and how to survive in desert conditions.

The whole convoy unknowingly circled around in the South Atlantic waters for about three days avoiding the U boats, going down almost to the Antarctic to get out of the way, and my word the seas were rough around the Cape of South Africa. We finally docked at Cape Town docks on the 12th December 1941.

A party of us went down to Nuremberg, famous for its wind surfing. It was there that a local business man took hold of my arm (and bear in mind we had been warned about civilians in case they were fifth columnists) and he told me to round up 39 men plus myself and he took us to a local hotel and provided a marvellous meal for us all, which we gladly accepted. He stated this was his way of helping the war efforts and we returned back to our ship at night, left with the thoughts of generosity from a total stranger!

It was my birthday on the 14th and when we went ashore for our leave, my dearest friend Victor Mortlock came shopping with me. I purchased a lovely watch. It was here that the local people used to meet up with the soldiers and take a car full of them home for meals. Scores and scores of natives arrived at the docks and began begging from us and the boys soon started throwing cigarettes, biscuits, money, anything that these poor people could have and even if that unfortunately landed in the water, the locals would quickly jump in to retrieve it.

The next day we didn't quite agree with what we were watching. We would see chauffeurs arriving at the dock side and three or four men would get inside and you could think what you liked. Were there girls inside the taxis taking them back home? We took a chance with two old ladies about 60 and 65 (where was our spirit of adventure, you might think!) but they asked us back to their home so off we went, Victor Mortlock, Joe and Arthur Brown and myself, the four of us whisked away on my birthday complete with new watch and all, via a very memorable trip up Table Mountain. The chauffeur took us up as far as possible and there were others up at the top admiring the view as well.

We enjoyed lovely panoramic views over Cape Town, breathtaking for us all. Then there was the excitement of the cable car trip back down the mountain. Never having seen such a thing before, aboard we climbed. The return downward trip took around a half an hour. Down to rejoin the chauffeur and the ride home with the two ladies continued. Those two dear old ladies took us back to their home and provided us with a really lovely meal and it was whilst standing on their veranda and listening to the six o'clock news that we heard the dreadful news of the sinking of the ships the "Repulse" and the "Prince of Wales".

H. M. S. "REPULSE".
LENGTH:- 794 Ft. BEAM:- 104 Ft. TONNAGE:- 37,400 TONS. COMPLEMENT:- 1,300.

THE REPULSE

PRINCE OF WALES

Although not part of our initial convoy, these two ships had been sunk by the Japanese and of the survivors, English and Americans included from those two wrecked ships, some men also still made it to Japan, only to be captured alongside me and held as prisoners of war.

After that we sat talking for a while with the family, and then they duly took us back to the "Mount Vernon" safe and sound at night.

These two dear folk promised to write home for us all. Whether they ever did I will never know. I will say they kept their promise, but due to boats and ships being blown apart by U boats during the ravages of the war perhaps their letters to our Parents never made it and my home had been split up and divided by the time I was to eventually get back to England.

It was at Cape Town, where some 26000 troops were waiting to be moved out, that we were to march for the last time with the 2nd Cambridgeshires band. An awesome sight and sound, on a beautifully clear and sunny day. The men in their scarlet and white tunics, all of whom were immaculately dressed and turned out, struck up playing their musical airs with their many polished brass instruments and drums, all gleaming in the sunlight. The sound of the band echoing across the dockland for all to hear loud and clear. There we started our final march past on the edge of Cape Town docks. It brought a lump to many a throat, mine in particular. Any band playing military music today is still my most favourite of tunes to listen to and the louder the better. It still makes the hairs on the back of my neck stand up!

Leaving Cape Town, we set sail into the Indian Ocean and after two days, just before Christmas, orders were given for the 53rd Infantry brigade to break from convoy formation and head for Mombasa, East Africa.

I recall the Captains words that the "Mount Vernon" was now "unaccompanied". Our ship now all alone in the open and dangerous seas, quite a chilling and sobering occasion after being in such a big company of men, with so many ships in the one convoy. Thoughts flashed through my mind. Would we be a sitting target, I wondered.

We arrived at Mombasa on Christmas day and I recall all the turkeys on board had gone off so had to be ditched overboard, so Christmas lunch 1941 consisted of bully beef and as much ice cream as you could manage... What a feast that was to be compared to the next few years' Christmas lunches to follow. Next day we were paraded into town in our gym kits and allowed to swim in the sea. We had two hours freedom and, yes, there were sharks nets in place in the sea to protect us.

On our way back to the ship we came across some people

selling fruit, so we purchased a load to take back on board with us. I recall a tiny little lad asking if he could carry it all back for us. I thought at the time that he looked too small to carry such a load but the others encouraged him to walk a little of the way back with us. Once back on board the “Mount Vernon” we soon tucked into our bounty and that was to be our Boxing Day treat.

One morning we, the same four boys who had been together up Table Mountain in Cape Town, had just gone into a coffee shop in Mombasa, this would be the day after Boxing Day, 27th December 1941. We had ordered a cucumber sandwich each, we hadn’t ordered any drinks at the time, when this man came up to us all in full uniform and he tapped me on the shoulder and said, with some authority I might add, "You go and get in that car outside", saying the same to my three mates. We were pretty dubious about him of course and asked how would we know which was his car, to which he replied, "My chauffeur is out there and he will see to you all."

We went outside and sure enough it was as the man said. The chauffeur opened the car door and in we got, trusting as ever. He reassured us that this strange uniformed man would be out in a minute. Out he came, hopped into the car with us and off we went. We drove on through the town and came to this great big place with iron gates and the native servants came out and opened up the gates for him. Up the private road we sped. We drove to this magnificent palace with high steps leading up to the doors. We pulled up and out came the footmen to open the car doors and out we all got and went up on top of the landing. We stood up there and he then said, "You will stay with us whilst you are in Mombasa." This man turned out to be none other than the Governor General himself.

He told to us that we could help ourselves to anything and have anything in his house that we wanted but there was one thing we were strictly not to touch, that was any alcohol. He went on to say "You will see us drinking whisky like water but you are not to touch any of it."

The Governor General’s wife came through with the children and we had some lemonade together. Then she said she would take us around the gardens and the youngest said whilst walking around with us "Mummy, that mans heels are wholly worn down", referring to me of course. At which her mother chastised her and told her she mustn't make comments like that about people. It's a wonder the Army hadn't picked me up about my shoes before but I had got away with it until this little girl spotted them.

A little while later the other little daughter said of me again, "Mummy, that man's stripes on his sleeve aren't straight, are they?" Agreed, they were a bit crooked. So this little girl also got told off, her mother telling her that they mustn't keep finding fault with us soldiers. However despite that initial embarrassment we had a lovely time there, tea together and everything else, truly genuine hospitality.

We were treated exceptionally well during the day by these lovely people, his wife and two lovely little daughters about the ages of eight and ten. This family took us to a church service and even to a safari park seeing the wild animals. Imagine our delight at seeing giraffe and tigers in the wild for the first time in our lives. He didn't pay to enter; neither did we, which was presumably because he was such a high ranking officer.

The chauffeur took us back at night to the "Mount Vernon", but the Governor General had already told us that at 2 o'clock tomorrow we would be collected again and true to his word we were duly collected for a trip out again. On the Sunday they took us to the Mombasa cathedral, again all the family along with us four soldiers. We went in there and partook of a lovely service. I didn't see any other soldiers in there and when it was over the minister came across to him, and the Governor General said to the minister, "I want to introduce you to my brothers from England." He himself being English from around Cheshire.

They took us back to the palace again for supper and I recall his wife saying, "Where shall we take the boys tomorrow, Daddy?" and he never answered and she repeated herself, "Where shall we take the boys tomorrow?" and he still never answered, to which she said "Oh! Well, you know something and you're not going to say. Will you please tell me what is going to happen to these boys!"

To which he replied, "I'm not going to say, but all I will say is may God bless them and take care of them wherever they go. Now it's time to go back to their boat." So out we came to go back to the ship and said our goodbyes, then back to the docks, saying farewell to the chauffeur, scampered up the gangplank and back on board the "Mount Vernon".

We had just settled into our bunks and at 12 o'clock at night the old engines started up with an almighty roar and out we sailed from Mombasa leaving behind many memorable hours. As we left the harbour there was a destroyer waiting to assist us on our passage and we had been at sea a day when a message came over the intercom. Everything went quiet and still. "Take notice we have heard from the War Office and we are destined for Singapore to try and stop the Japanese from coming down further into Malaya."

Well our hearts sank! We had at worst thought we would be fighting against Rommel in the desert, as we had been training earlier for desert warfare. So it was now clear to us all, whilst waiting in Mombasa the War Office still hadn't made up their minds what to do with the 53rd Infantry but by now we were sailing away, making our way via India and onto Malaya to stop the Japanese, who were advancing at an alarming pace. This war was now all too much of a reality.

The following days passed very quickly and the "Mount Vernon" finally docked at Singapore Harbour on 13th January 1942. On docking we hastily disembarked, making our way ashore complete with all our equipment. This was it, war against the Japanese.

CHAPTER TWO

JANUARY 1942 SINGAPORE

"DAYS BEFORE MY CAPTIVITY"

I was in captivity at the hands of the Japanese from February 15th 1942 to an unknown date in 1945, so allow me to tell you of my experiences throughout that time.

The "Mount Vernon" docked. We had arrived on Singapore Island on 13th January 1942 and were given three days to prepare for battle. Back at Crewe something must have gone dreadfully wrong with the loading of our Bren guns and carriers, sports gear etc, as none of this shipload could now be found. Another vessel was quickly drafted in to us but their equipment was painted beige, presumably ready for the desert warfare against Rommel. What a setback. So in a short space of time we repainted our fresh Bren guns and carriers to a dark green colour, ready for jungle camouflage, cleaned and checked our weapons and made ready for what was to come. We had already heard of the dreadful fate of other ships and it was apparent to us that this Japanese fighting force was a scary bunch of men to deal with, let alone fight. The very word Jap in those days conjured up fear and trepidation, emotions the likes of which I hadn't even begun to think of back home, but here we were in an all too real world that was falling apart. Country against country, man against man, was this God's intention for us all to go about killing each other? I think not.

TAKEN BEFORE BEING CAPTURED

Before taken prisoner I fought in Malaya in the fierce battle of Batu Pahat. I was in charge of the Bren gun carrier. Being in command I had three men working alongside with me in the carrier.

In the midst of a fierce battle a major of the Royal Artillery stopped our tank and asked for a lift further up the line. He climbed on board the carrier and about ten minutes after we set off, my gunner, William Peacock of Willingham, Cambridgeshire, slapped me on my head and pointed back to where the major had been sitting, I then saw that the top of the major's head had been blown completely off, obviously by a Japanese sniper. What kind of a war was this going to be? We were about to well and truly find out over the next months and years to come.

A few days later my gunner Willy was hit twice on the side of his head so he was taken back to Headquarters First Aid post. Two days after that my driver (Rutterford from Barton, Cambs) was hit right through the ear, so back he went to HQ for first aid... all this was whilst fighting in the first few days for Batu Pahat.

One occasion I was working alongside another Bren gun commander and his team, like myself (whose names I will withhold to protect their families). At about midday our officer, Captain Page, with Sergeant Legge came to us both saying we were to be prepared to take the two carriers and travel back to Brigade Head Quarters at Bahesslong at around 6 o'clock in the evening for some special mission. Whether it was to take something with us, collect some information or stores, we had no idea at this point as we were not told.

At 5 o'clock that evening Legge came to me to say things had all been altered. He didn't know why, only that the other carrier commander and his team of men would go alone and I would not be going with my carrier and crew. The only reasonable offer of explanation was that their carrier was a faster type than my one. His carrier was fitted with a Rolls Royce engine whilst mine had a Ford. Never mind. I was disappointed at the time, in fact looking forward to the trip back, being out of the fighting line for an hour or two, but we had to obey orders and that was that.

Sadly as it transpired later, none of these men ever came back! We were told the next morning that the men had achieved their orders and were almost safely back to our camp when they were ambushed at a road block. The Japs used to drop trees to block the roads. The commander was killed when he got out of his carrier to check and look for a way around the blockade. He was caught and had both his hands severed off by the Japs. The two men with him were killed in their carrier itself, presumably shot. We lost three good men right quickly that night. There but for the grace of God went I and my Bren gun team of men.

We were being heavily attacked and still trying to defend the port area we were in. Two carriers ahead of me made it safely over one road block. With trees in our path, I shouted to my driver to slow down and put the carrier into low gear and creep over the fallen trees as the men ahead had done. But alas he knew best and went ahead far too quickly, keeping the carrier in a higher gear. He quickly swerved to go around the trees at the edge of the roadway. Sure enough, it was swamp-like ground and over we went. The engine was screaming away like crazy, every Jap in the vicinity would now know we were in deep trouble. I shouted it was now too late, so abandon and take cover.

I regrettably lost my carrier on the attempted withdrawal from Batu Pahat. I was forced to abandon it owing to the carrier becoming stuck on soft ground. It went over on to its offside under intensive fierce fire from the Japs. Fortunately for us, the fire was coming from the one side and the vehicle on its side now gave us protection to quickly get out and make a dive for cover. Many vehicles were fast becoming abandoned, their work over, ruined and of no further use in saving our lives or of those of the local natives we had come to defend. Armament was strewn everywhere and quickly rendered worthless with the might of the onslaught that followed from the Japs.

There was extensive fighting going on all around us, men were being seriously wounded and we had many fatalities. The situation was now immensely frightening to us all. The smoke-filled darkened skies lit up with the flashes from the guns, the noise was deafening from the blasts of guns and rifles. Grown men screaming in agony. We were now truly fighting for our very lives. Men struck down had to be left to die where they fell, afraid and alone.

Civilians too were making a dash for safety where and when they could, almost quite literally carrying their homes on their backs, taking with them what ever they could manage to carry. Columns of people walking away from their homeland, others scattering like sheep in all directions, driven from their own homes by the invading forces of the Japanese. It was total chaos. Thousands didn't make it, of that I'm sure. What buildings stood were soon blown apart, Japs destroying anything and everything in and around the area we were fighting for.

We, that is my new driver Freddie Room and new gunner Joe Brown from Prickwillow, Cambridgeshire, had to make a dive for cover into the malaria drain to escape the firing, by this time the order had already been given "Every man for himself." This order received and clearly understood, we decided to make for the sea by using our compass and common sense, and it took us some four to five days to reach the coast. I know now that the distance was around seventeen miles.

After seventeen miles trekking and hacking through virgin jungle for five days, we eventually caught up with fifty soldiers, all members of the 2nd Cambs. I saw a local kampong across the swamp and said I would go and fill up our water bottles as I could see a water tank nearby. My mate said he would go over instead whilst we gave him cover. On the way over to the water tank he was challenged by someone calling his name, which startled him. Once he realised it was our own officer who asked him what he was doing and why and who he was with. The man with me replied he was with Corporal Lockwood, to which the officer told him not to be so stupid; Lockwood was killed on Sunday morning. But there I stood, waiting for some fresh cold water.

So that earlier group of men were something pleased to see us all, when we stood up. We all assembled the best we could and laid in waiting under atap trees for three days until we were rescued and taken off by the Royal Navy. Someone asked if anyone knew Morse code; someone said he vaguely did, so at night he used to signal out to sea hoping one of our ships might flash back. Alas, nothing for three nights, when hooray, at last back flashed a message, "Stay put, pick you up in 24 hours, ten men at a time." Sure enough, a boat pulled in as close as it could under cover of darkness, took off ten men, put them on the frigate, then that took them off to a troop carrier out in deeper waters. Five trips took place and I was on the last boat, dangling from the end of a rope that had safely taken the previous forty-nine men safely, me a non swimmer floundering away at the end of the now untied line but we were all away… free men at last!

Once aboard the troop ship the captain gave us all a drink and told us to drink it all up. We didn't need any encouraging, not having eaten or even had any water for seven days, so gulp it down we did. We were desperately thirsty and tired men, and you can guess the rest, we slept like logs, that's navy rum for you. Unbelievably after 24 hours we were placed back on Singapore Island again and straight back into the midst of the fighting once more!

There we quickly dug in to defend Singapore, but the fighting was too intense. We were heavily out numbered by the Japanese so were forced to withdraw from our position on the north shore. After heavy shelling and small arms fire we were told after a certain amount of time to withdraw to the cemetery, I believe Buka Timah. When you are ordered to "fix bayonets" then rest assured the end is pretty nigh for someone, one to one hand combat fighting. I trembled from head to toe but obeyed orders and fought on. Thank the Lord I didn't have to use my own bayonet on anyone.

There we fought fierce battles all Saturday, through the night and into Sunday. It was the two longest days of my life. You could see the Japs scurrying around, running and charging at you low, using the ground for cover. I was informed the Japs were bringing up a three-inch gun to use to wipe us all out, and so I informed our soldiers in my section of this news. One named Slim Mason got stuck into the Japs. He defiantly held his ground and kept his guns trained so tightly onto them. He went really mad with that Bren gun, picking them off like flies, so effectively that their three-inch gun couldn't be set up and used on us. A truly brave man indeed. He clearly could have sacrificed his own life to help protect as many of us as he could. All of this and only to be told at 2.30 pm on the Sunday afternoon that at 4pm we were to lay down our arms and surrender to the Japanese on the 15th February 1942. Us surrender to the Japs... never, or so I thought at the time!!

Whilst taking one of the much-needed ten minute breaks

from the front line firing, I was talking together with my best mate Victor Mortlock and he was asking about the watch I had bought in Cape Town.

Wanting to admire the watch at close quarters I opened the sweat band on my wrist and removed it for him to closely inspect. He was always messing about one way or the other despite all the happenings of war and he pretended to throw the watch away. Alas, the joke was on me. The watch flew out of his hand and promptly catapulted over the hedge and landed in the neighbouring cemetery, which we were totally forbidden to enter. I believe the make of watch was a Service watch. Some service it gave me, all of three or four months. He was gutted and so was I, but it was an accident, albeit a stupid one and still the battle of war ensued around us.

Our company sergeant major had already threatened me that if I didn't order my section of three men to surrender I would be court-martialled, something I suspect he must have repeated to many a proud British soldier at the time. I do recall not long after that laying my rifle on the pile along with about 50 others. All of us having sabotaged our weapons before disposing of them. We also buried our razors and knives. You see this early on into what was to be our captivity; we had already been told and threatened that our throats would soon be cut!

The next day early at about 7am the Japs came in to us in very large numbers and frisked us for guns, etc. I was amazed by the size of those Japs. You see, not all Japanese are small so-and-sos. Being heavily armed with machine guns, swords, bamboo poles, they, the mighty Japanese Imperial Army whom we had feared meeting face to face, were now indeed and unquestionably, an imposing fighting force to reckon with.

After a day or so our medical officers and orderlies sorted through and around the area we had been fighting in, searching and scouring the area for dead bodies, more importantly too in searching and looking for our wounded soldiers. Before we were to be moved further up country, our officer came across to me and said that he wanted to congratulate me. I said "Whatever for, Sergeant?" He went on to relay, that during that search 26 dead Japs had been found around the area outside our gun section that Slim was holding. So to this day I am totally convinced that he had a hand in thwarting their particular progress and in the process saved our souls.

You see the high number of Japs that died in that particular spot would have been under direct orders from Tojo himself, to set up and use this field gun to blast us out of oblivion, and if he said "Fight to the death" that is what those Japanese soldiers would have done. They would not have retreated; they would have sent even more Japs in to kill us off, even under such intense fire from Slim. I never did keep in touch with Slim, from then on we were split up and he has now since departed this world, but without a doubt I would say another true saint has gone on to heaven.

On the Tuesday we were force marched by the Japs further up country to the Roberts Barracks in Changhi where other men had already been rounded up inside. There I first witnessed the senselessness and heartlessness of the Japs. They pushed us all into the barrack block by one door, Japs standing with fixed bayonets were brutally forcing us into this absolutely crowded barrack room, which I suppose would have normally held about 600 personnel.

The Japs literally forced thousands of us to go in through this one door at gun point. Consequently we walked over our own wounded, dead and dying soldiers already trapped inside. The smell and the language was indescribable, something I will never forget as long as I may live. This was to be the first of many prodding's with a Japanese bayonet. I was stabbed along with many others who refused to trample over their dead and dying colleagues but we soon learnt we simply had no choice in the matter, being at the hands of our captors, already witnessing the unlawful killings of anyone refusing to carry out their orders. We were eventually pushed and prodded forward, trampling over and crushing our own men's bones and bodies, many of them dying under our own feet. I cannot express my emotions now but then it was extreme disbelief, shock, anger, sorrow. Heartbreaking events happening so early on, that are as clear to me now as they were over sixty years ago, clearly still all too vivid in my mind.

We just could not breathe in there, so we pushed open an exit door and spilled out onto the lawn and laid there for days and days. Some men were even dug in into sandpits. There was just nowhere to get under cover from the scorching sun which caused the sweat to pour off you and then the rain which at times was torrential. Adverse weather conditions the likes of which we had not encountered back home in England.

After landing on Singapore Island and being taken prisoner by the Japs, we still had our army rations with us. All the main stores were quickly raided mainly by the Japs and indeed by our own men. Because nothing had prepared our own people for this, we had no supplies of food whatsoever as back-up with us. So our own officers came around to us and told us, that as we still had our haversack rations, we were to be very careful how we eked it out. We were allowed to have a quarter of a biscuit twice a day. These biscuits were about four inches square, not as tasty as today's off the supermarket shelf, but purpose made hard biscuits, supposedly packed with nutrients and vitamins for the forces to eat. So that is how we survived for food in the early days of our captivity.

Robert Barracks was where my best mate Victor Mortlock lay seriously ill for the best part of a month, unable to stomach any of the eastern food rations given to him. We nearly lost him on this occasion but miraculously he pulled through that time. I suggested that we held a little gospel service. This was totally forbidden. I remember Mort saying, "Can we sing 'Fight the good fight'?" Lance Corp. Thomas from Whepstead gave a short bible reading. This short religious ceremony helped many through those earlier harrowing scenes.

It was at Roberts Barracks, Changhi, where we still had a trickle of our haversack rations left, that the Japs started to bring the rice in. Of course we British boys hadn't encountered this type of rice back home (unlike today where you can feast in England and taste almost any nation's food, but this was unheard of in those days). So what was this rice how was it to be cooked, what would it taste like? Well some boys could eat it and some most definitely could not stomach it at all... well at least not in the early days... later it was rice or nothing... and nothing meant death!! Oh! how I yearned for a milk rice pudding with currants in, which mother made for us all.

After three months at Roberts Barracks in Changhi, where

for the best part of those three months we sat, stood and slept out in the open, no roof whatsoever over our heads and no protection from what ever the weather decided to throw at us. We were force-marched over fourteen miles during the day but in torrential rain to Singapore Siam Road Camp to do any kind of work.

Any vehicles that did accompany the march were soon churning away in the mud, getting stuck, being pushed or pulled out; men were squelching their way along the pathways. It was a tiresome journey but we were relatively speaking still fairly fit men, although many men were now already looking very ragged with their worn-out clothes and shoes that had seen better days. So with toes poking out of worn down shoes or bare-footed, on we marched. Rations were very, very poor by now. We had finished our army rations and were now being made to eat their rice.

To get the best results from the cookhouse, some Dutchmen came over to us from Java and they took over the cooking for all the prisoners. They tried their very best to make the rice as tasty as they could with odd bits of fish or vegetables and fruit. It was at this time when the Dutchmen arrived from Java, and these men were used to rice in their diets back home, so they naturally knew how to prepare it, that they set about taking over total control of the cooking.

Boiled rice with scraps of this and that, some of fish which resembled stickle backs, courtesy of the River Kwai no doubt. Some vegetables, which didn't resemble anything I could recognize from my father's vegetable plot back home in Cockfield. Anything that could be had was hacked up and put into the rice to make it as palatable as humanly possible, this along with some tinned fish that was found and pinched at the docks and quickly secreted back to the cooks. The docks were in fact crammed full of stores including food, but however we were not to see any of that. Bet your bottom dollar the Japs fed well though!

Soon we were to learn to exist on about a handful of bland rice given twice a day if we were lucky. We used to queue up with our dixies and were given just over half a cup of rice, twice a day as I say, if you were lucky, once if you were not quick enough though. Amazingly out of all the things that I had pinched I managed to keep my spoon and mess tin throughout my captivity.

I joined a group of fifty-five men out of the hundreds that were captured; these were mainly men from the 2nd Cambridgeshires. We came down off the cemetery and stood on a corner of the plot. That first night an officer instructed Leggy to form a stick guard. This turned out to be our last guard for the British army. Leggy said to me, "What on earth are we going to do, Sid, if the Japs come after us, mate?" to which I recall saying something like throw the sticks at them and run like blazes. We didn't fancy being shot this early on anyway.

CHAPTER THREE

APRIL/MAY 1942

BEHEADING OF CIVILIANS

I recall vividly the whistling of "Colonel Bogey", a memorable tune and despite the rain we marched as only the Brits can march. This time we were force-marched by the Japs from Roberts Barracks to Siam Road camp. The Japs had a job with their little legs to keep up with us, some even on bicycles struggling along in the sludge and mud on the roads.

On arrival at Siam Road Camp, we found that many huts had previously been erected and used by the British forces. These huts were to become our homes for several weeks. It was in this camp that Mort found a gold coin. He found it on a ledge in a wash room. It certainly helped us two out nicely, enabling us to barter for some extra food from the locals

Buka Timah cemetery was eventually to become our surrender ground and some four months later, one morning on parade (tenco) a Jap came up and muttered that he wanted san ma jradosha, or in other words three men and one must be a lorry driver, to go along with him. Joe Brown and his brother Arthur, both great lads from Prickwillow, Cambridgeshire, said to me, "Come on, Sid, you can drive and we will come with you."

I can still see the Jap's face as it lit up with a huge grin as he marched us off down through the army stores. Cars, vans, lorries, vehicles everywhere and everything English until we came to the American depot and here he stopped beside a massive great big six-wheel left-hand-drive American lorry, with a winch and pulley on the front. The Jap pushed me as if to say you get in and drive the thing. I was scared absolutely stiff. If I couldn't start the blessed lorry it would have been bash, bash, bash for me that is for certain, but luckily and to my amazement it fired first time. So off we went, my two mates as well, not forgetting the Jap who stood right close to me during the journey. Me, driving an American six wheeler! Who would have thought of it? What would the Goldings make of me now?

We went on down past rows and rows of every type of implement you could imagine until we came to the chains and the ropes department, whereupon he ordered Joe and Arthur to put jit nee, which was thirteen chains and ropes on board our lorry and off we went, the Jap poking me as to which way he wanted us to go.

We drove on and as we turned into the middle of Singapore onto the Jahore Road, Making, the streets were busy with mixed nationalities all going about their business. This is when I saw a sight I'll never forget. There were three wire ropes strung out across the street and each wire had about twenty heads of human beings hung on them, these being beheaded civilians.

I said to Joe and Arthur, "What the blazes (words to that effect) is this?"

The Jap punched me in the back and said, "Pinchy, pinchy." I knew from that moment what he meant. Those unfortunate victims had been caught stealing and looting, and this was their fate.

All that day we went backwards and forwards under those heads. The road was awash with blood, but we had a task to do which took us almost down to the naval barracks to collect all the abandoned cars, some of which had hardly a scratch on them; others were dumped or smashed up. We hauled them out of ditches, off the side of the tracks wherever they had been abandoned and attached them somehow to our lorry with the ropes and chains. Incidentally a lovely MG sports car was taken back to one of the camps by a Jap Officer, so not all vehicles made it for scrap iron.

Arthur was in his glory seeing what was left in those abandoned vehicles, cigarettes, money, biscuits... whatever he could lay his hands on he took. There were plenty of pickings to be had, as many vehicles had been abandoned in haste. Because of the fighting as civilians became trapped, so they fled into the nearby jungle, leaving their prized possessions behind them, items which the Japs swiftly rounded up.

Joe attached the ropes and chains to the wrecks and we gave our Jap guard some cigarettes to keep him quiet. When we had a load of about six or seven cars on board we dragged them full pelt down to the docks where some POWs were waiting with bulldozers and dinkham diggers. They then compressed the cars into moveable bales and then the POW with the magnetic crane lifted and placed the heaps of scrap iron onto a boat destined for Japan, no doubt to be made into aircraft parts or ammunition for their war effort.

Back we would go for more loads of wrecked cars under the civilians' heads and this task lasted about two days, finally returning the big old American lorry to its so-called depot.

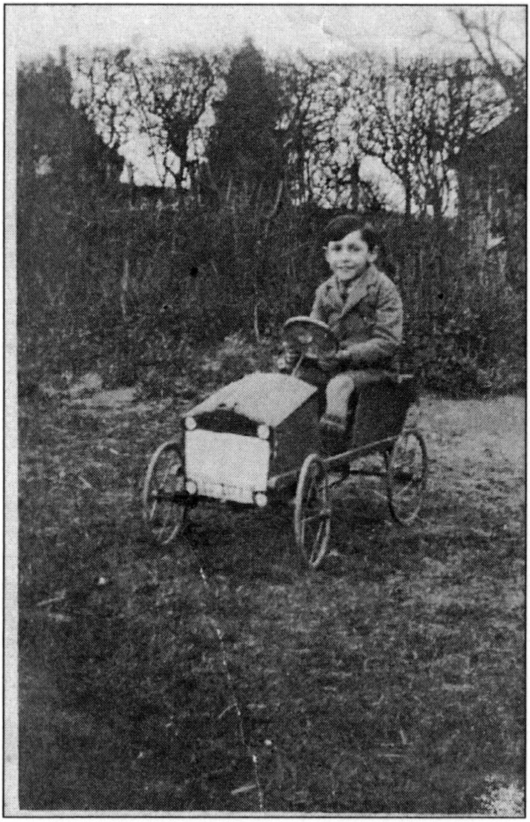

A FAR CRY FROM MY FIRST SET OF WHEELS BACK HOME

After that we would be put onto another job like repairing wires, up poles. Maybe this was GPO, General Post Office work of a kind, no doubt reconnecting Singapore with the outside world again. We had plenty of tasks lined up for us repairing anything that the war had already rendered useless.

We were put to work from Siam Road Camp, taken out in various gangs of men to do all manner of work, still under guard, even doing a bit of gardening for the camp. Japs still stood watch over us, but I hasten to add the Japs had the first pickings from our vegetable patch.

Lots of time was spent working in the dock area as well, although I didn't join that particular party of men in those earlier days. The officers chose selected people who were light-fingered and nifty, if you know my meaning, as they would be the ones who dared to get us the extra pickings and supplies back discreetly to camp, anything stolen and anyhow they could manage it all without being caught. Brave acts on their behalf but a risky and deadly game to play nonetheless.

CHAPTER FOUR

MAY 1942

HORNETS' NEST AT SIAM ROAD CAMP

Matters were deteriorating rapidly for us prisoners now and as one of the many punishments during our hard labour, the Japs would place their swill bins of waste food quite close to our huts, hoping of course that we would go and scavenge from them. Alas, the local Chinese folk were hungry too. They beat us to the pickings, where upon they were severely beaten and their loved ones raped in full view of us prisoners. It was truly heart-breaking, scenes we were physically forced to fully watch and witness. Hence they all took the beatings that were originally intended for us had we stolen the Jap's waste food. It was hard, mind you, to resist such scraps though, as food was in desperate shortage to us as POWs by now.

One day a Jap was rummaging around in the undergrowth and found a hornets' nest on a stretch that I was working on. They poked fun at the nest all day long hoping someone would be stung and around 5pm on this day, a Jap rammed his bayonet into the nest; you can guess the rest! Yes... lucky Sidney, I was stung just under my left eye. My mate Wally Spencer (Holland on Sea) saw what happened and quickly rolled me down onto the ground and sucked out the hornet's sting. Alas, it immediately swelled up and closed my eye, which remained closed for about a week. You see, we had nothing with us to treat anything like a sting of this nature. The Japs thought it was hilarious; it made their day.

I landed up in sick bay and after about a week I returned to the working party, which at that particular time was set to work on building a shrine for the Japanese to use in celebration...

because they were going to win this war, or so they thought at the time. After about three weeks I went totally blind and was really scared stiff. This was I think about the month of June. It was then we were given our first postcard to send home to our family. Because I was blind, my best mate Victor Mortlock (Wickhambrook) filled mine in for me, then held my hand and helped me to sign my name. My words at that time to him were "If only my poor old mother could see me now, more to the point just what would she think or say?"

Victor replied, "I don't suppose they will ever receive these cards Sid." They apparently did but it was to be some two years later. Incidentally I recently read in my local newspaper where one such POW post card written at the same time as mine was due to go under the auctioneer's hammer, expecting to raise approximately £300. A far cry from being penniless in a foreign jungle when the cards were written.

The Red Cross had managed to get some food parcels into Siam Road Camp. One parcel between 13 men, but these were handed over to the cookhouse staff officials and therefore shared out between as many as was humanly possible.

Out of those meagre food parcels I somehow managed to get hold of enough vitamins to help me to have my eyesight gradually restored, thank God.

One man, George Hurrell, who lives in my home town of Bury St Edmunds, was working away with me on the railway bed towards the Chungkai cutting. On return home and years later, I met George of all places in Bury Hospital. Unfortunately I was about the first returning POW to enter my home town hospital. One morning as I roused who should be lying in the bed right next to me but George. After our initial chat this gave me the chance to ask him why it was he never seemed to go down in health and strength as rapidly as the rest of us boys did, whilst working away on the railway line.

Well, he proceeded to explain, that whilst working towards the cutting, it was his duty every day to go to the Jap cook house and to bring back about sixteen full dixies of food for the Jap guards to have for their lunch and that was as much as he could carry.

A big responsibility in itself, ensuring he was not late back, not spilling any of it on his return. We used to see George go off maybe an hour before our ten-minute break was sounded and he would come back laden with these dixies around his neck, his waist, any way he could possibly carry them. I noticed then back in the jungle, how well he looked compared to many, and I expect several other men must have wondered the same, but said nothing about his appearance at the time. This went on for weeks and weeks and bear in mind we hardly use to speak to anyone on the lines, the Japs seldom accepted any talking amongst the POWs at labour, so now my chance had come whilst lying beside him in hospital, to ask him why it was?

Having asked him why he looked so well compared to us... he just burst our laughing and said nothing more about it!

We both improved, left the hospital and went about our homely duties, coincidentally both attempting to be lorry drivers. Only to meet up with George several years later, when he said "Sid, there is something I want to tell you. You always asked me why did I look so well in Chungkai. The fact is when I collected those dixies for the Japs' lunch, on the way back I used to drink up all the gravy."

To which I replied, "My goodness, man, you took a considerable risk. What if they had noticed it was short rations." He burst out laughing yet again and told me not to be so naive... to this I laughed heartily too... yes... he admitted he had piddled in all the dixies to bring them back full to the brim again.

There was a ladies' meeting at our local church recently, talking about Long Brackland, and the area of town George now lives. If I had known I'd have loved to have been there and had the courage to tell... how those ladies would have laughed to know of this mans colourful and funny escapade. Well done George...!

CHAPTER FIVE

JUNE/JULY 1942

Buka Timah/Singapore Island

SIGNING OF NON ESCAPE PAPERS

It was at Buka Timah that the Imperial Japanese Army issued the "non escape papers" to our Senior officers and due to all POWs flatly refusing to sign such papers, around 17000 men (yes, seventeen thousand men) were herded onto a type of tennis court area. This area was secured and heavily fenced off, plus it had Jap guards patrolling all around it. They were all heavily armed, with machine guns trained straight at us and would not have hesitated to use them, probably itching to use them and presumably clearly instructed by their commanders to kill all of us if our officers failed to sign the non escape papers.

On joining the army, it was clearly explained to us all, that if we were unfortunately captured, anywhere or at anytime, we had to attempt to escape back to our units.

The Japanese army would be fully aware of these instructions and therefore aware we would intend to escape. Hence "non escape papers" were drawn up for our Senior officers to sign, on our behalf. Declaring that we would make no attempt to escape at all.

Imagine the sight all those 17000 men having to stay on this one pitch crammed to capacity, shoulder to shoulder, staying there in the boiling sun for three very hot days and nights with just two dixies of water, no food, no sanitation and dysentery was already rife by this time. Many men were being squashed literally to their death and left where they lay until we were permitted to give them a decent burial. Death was already sadly becoming all too regular and familiar a sight.

We had to stay there herded worse than you would dare to treat an animal, until our Senior officers said they would sign the non escape papers... after a lot of blackmail on behalf of the Japs and threats to murder some of the POWs in cold blood and even to bring the entire tally of sick men out of their local hospital beds to join us in the compound, the Senior officers reluctantly and eventually did sign "under duress". Hence we were to be released from the compound.

With our spirits now totally down and feeling completely dejected and demoralised we were soon set to work, in forced labour gangs, building their shrine at Buka Timah Golf Course.

From proud soldier to humbled slave on the signing of papers. From now on to be looked upon by the Japs as cowards for surrendering in the first place. An expendable work force that they could now do with as they pleased. Many a Jap took open pleasure in the way he dealt with a prisoner and over the following years they put their training into very good use against us POWs. Their plans could now be fulfilled, well and truly executed and if we didn't oblige by obeying their orders, then simply they would execute us as well.

Life as a proud soldier was rapidly changing. We were now prisoners of war; our morale was spiralling downwards and fast. Shaving became irregular and beards soon took hold and appeared everywhere on weary men's faces throughout the camp.

You could have a hair cut by a barber called Reeve if you had enough money. Mostly we would just hack bits and pieces off each others hair with a sharpened-up army knife. The rugged and tangled look soon took hold on the majority of us prisoners.

If our government could see us all now what would they think? Is this what serving your King and Country was all about? Yes it is, but wars and fighting still goes on today, so I would ask what have we learnt from the previous two disastrous world wars. When you watch your TV screens the answer is simply that we have learnt precious little in valuing our lives and all that surrounds us, our country and above all our freedom. I wished I had my freedom back, right there and then at Buka Timah but it had been taken from me.

Now I was to do my best to survive the ordeal ahead as a prisoner held at the hands of the Japanese, so that I could return to my homeland and family safe and sound. It was soon to become all too apparent that only the strongest and luckiest would survive.

CHAPTER SIX

JULY/AUGUST 1942

BREAKING UP THE ROADS ON SINGAPORE ISLAND

There were hundreds and hundreds of prisoners, working away with pick axes and chunkles. Any type of hand tool implement but absolutely nothing at all mechanical for us to use. The Japs made sure this was to be forced labour in every sense of the word. I can only ask you to imagine the scene for yourselves as we worked on, breaking up tarmac and cement roads and moving any vegetation in our path.

One day I was working hard, being prodded and bashed at as usual, and in the one day I was working so hard that I accidentally broke FOUR pick axe handles. The Japs were absolutely mad with me. I mean they went literally mad with anyone that broke or damaged any mortal piece of working apparatus. My mates said, "'For goodness sake' don't break any more they'll kill you if you do."

I replied, "They won't kill me." I was still very determined about that fact despite what was going on around us.

Men in the gang just went on bantering back that I was wrong and would be killed. However, I cracked the fifth pick axe handle and fortunately lived to tell this tale

As we continued through the days breaking up this tarmac-hardcore base with these pick axes, there were hundreds and hundreds of us men in a chain gang effect. Some working with the baskets clearing the rubble away, these baskets had two handles, one man each side taking rubble away to another part of the site across the lake, up the hill to another area where the Japs were building a shrine, or rather I should say the prisoners were building their shrine for them. So we continued back and forth queuing up to refill these baskets time and time again, day after day and from dawn until dusk... many men now totally barefoot with only a loin cloth for protection. All shoes and most clothing had simply rotted away or been stolen; hats that still remained were indeed treasured by their owners.

Whilst working on the building of the shrine which was situated on a hill, the Japs ordered 50 men to pull a steam roller up the hill and believe it or not, then order 50 other men to pull it back DOWN again... what logic but funny to witness at the time and of course no one spilt the beans on this escapade!!

Even funnier still to a point, this steam engine was driven by an Australian and for a long period of time he dutifully drew two gallons of petrol daily to run this steam engine. Little did the Japs know about water driven "steam engines". Unfortunately this Australian's con was twigged by a Jap and his petrol con was rumbled. Alas no one saw him again. I'll leave you to decide upon his fate.

At 10 o'clock in the morning we had a ten-minute break and at 3 o'clock in the afternoon we had another ten-minute break. Now tea was produced from a five-gallon drum, no milk or sugar of course, just boiled tea. If you were near enough to the drum you would be lucky enough to get a drink, drop down where you stood, drink up in the allotted time of ten minutes, because after that you made sure you were back in the chain gang and hard at work. An old klaxon signalled the start and finish of these breaks and we looked just like a lot of ants working away scurrying back and forth.

So the work continued breaking the tarmac, clearing the rubble along the river bank, up that hill back over the bridge and so on. On one occasion as we were coming back over one of the bridges Lt. Clancy said, "Oi! you two" being George Baker from Haslingfield who was nick-named "Basher" and myself. He had spotted that we hadn't made it on one of the tea breaks to get our drink so he called us out of the chain gang and into a jungle clearing where he was brewing up and was about to give us a drink, when in came or should I say in charged, the Japs. They went ballistic and were hopping mad. They were going to shoot us and everything else there and then. The officer tried to reason with them but they weren't going to have any of it or even attempt to listen to him, they just wanted to dish out some more punishment to anyone and this time it happened to be George and myself in the firing line, so to speak. Tea was the last thing on their minds.

Having committed this so-called terrible crime in the Japs' eyes, George and I were made to stand to attention in the boiling sun for four hours. They placed us high up on a mound of earth standing some eight to ten feet in the air and we were not allowed to speak to anyone or to ask for anything. We had to remain motionless and totally silent for as long as they thought appropriate. This would ensure the punishment was made to fit the crime. After about 30 minutes the breeze blew my hat straight off. No way was I allowed to pick it up or anyone else for me for that matter, so I had to be British and stick it out, the boiling sun pouring down on me. Standing to attention made you dizzy and numb, you had that... not with it feeling... creeping over you, swaying to say the least. Incoherent, but still underneath the surface, there was a strong feeling of determination to beat this at all costs.

If anyone attempted to go near the hat to rescue it for me they were sworn at or hit out at. This mound of earth was smack bang in the middle of the working area, to add to our embarrassment or so they thought, so as the boys used to go past they would try to cheer us both us by whispering and saying things like "Only about two hours to go and we'll slit the Japs' throats for you later".

God alone knows how we both stuck to attention for so long motionless in that intense heat, beads of sweat running down our bodies, until we looked liked we had just emerged from a shower, but we did endure the torture for well over three long hours then the Japs stood us down. The first thing I did was to rush and grab my hat from where it landed and put that on. Then they ordered Lt. Clancy our officer to give us a hard boiled egg and a cup of tea each. We thought it was over but then they ordered us up onto the mound again to stand to attention in the sun for the remainder of the time.

What effect this had on our ailing health I just don't know

as the temperature was simply scorching hot and all this dished out because we had a caring officer trying to do his best for his men and all that over a cup of so-called tea, I ask you...

It was later during the month of August that we were ordered to go to Thailand to a "holiday camp" or so they said, but at last we were moving on. We were allowed to take all remaining gear with us and we all hoped to go to pastures new and better things, with easier times ahead!!

CHAPTER SEVEN

AUGUST 1942

EN ROUTE TO A HOLIDAY CAMP, BAN PONG, THAILAND

On the move yet again; another beleaguered camp left behind, this time we were marched from Siam Road Camp to Singapore Station. As we arrived at Singapore Station en route to Thailand, we thought of luxury carriages like those for me back at Bury St Edmunds station, maybe a plush seat to rest upon and a window to gaze from to at least admire this wonderful terrain we felt we would never leave. What a shock, not so. About twenty totally enclosed steel goods trucks awaited us, with three heavily armed Japanese guards to 31 POWs per truck, all ready and lined up for our onward journey.

These trucks were already baking hot to the touch and were to be our transportation for the next four, very long torturous days and nights, as we travelled about 1000 miles to Ban Pong. Scarcely enough room inside for every man to even sit down, no seats as we eagerly hoped for, just the hot dusty floor of the truck. So it was evident that hard and back aching hours lay ahead. Thus we eventually took it in turns standing, squatting whatever you could manage inside this mobile prison of a railway truck.

STEEL TRUCKS THAT WERE AT OUR DISPOSAL

The Jap guards were ordering us to mount the carriages. They couldn't count so Sgt. Jugg said to me, "Sid, we'll go with two men short so that we can get a little more space and air." All went well until we crossed over the border from Malaya into Thailand, then the Thai guard wanted to know how many men were entering their country as in fact they were opposed to Japs entering into their country at all, so they ordered us all out of the carriages and counted us... Thai guards can count!!

On finding out our truck only had 29 POWs instead of the 31 we were instructed to take at the start of the journey, the Thais told the Japs, who immediately turned on Juggy and myself, being in charge of the truck load of men and accused us of letting two men escape en route.

Two Japs with fixed bayonets forced us up against the brick wall at the edge of the platform and demanded that we tell them who had escaped and where it happened, their bayonets already making a good impression on our ragged skin. Juggy remarked to me, "Sid, if they are going to kill us I hope they shoot us as I don't fancy being bayoneted to death."

Being so close and face to face with these very irate angry men was very chilling indeed. It brought memories surging back of when I was told to "fix bayonets" before our surrender.

Mercifully I didn't use mine on one of them, now I prayed God's hand would hold them back from using their bayonets on us.

Juggy, with mixed language, asked, "Can any of you b's speak English?"

Lo and behold one big Thai man came forward and said to us two "Yes I'm a Thai business man. I can speak perfect English."

So Juggy retorted, "Tell the b' Jap we left Singapore with 29 men and not 31." Still the Japs argued with us for more than an hour until Juggy said to the Thai, "Tell that Jap to ring up Singapore and see how many men went through the turnstile". After a further hour the message came: 483 and not 485 as the Japs originally counted. So eventually we really were let off the hook, as it was no joke looking at the 12 inches of pure sparkling steel all this while which these two furious Japs were itching to use on us two POWs.

At the very start of this journey we were all told we were going to a holiday camp and to take all the sporting gear we could handle. Six POWs even took their piano, as they too believed things were going to get easier not the reverse, and because at that stage we were totally unaware of the preparation of "the railway of death", as it turned out to be.

If you can imagine the choking stench rising inside these stifling hot carriages with men lying in their own excrement. Many too ill to move to the doorway, where men would be held by comrades, whilst the train was travelling, rear end out of the door to do their ablutions, or be sick, whatever and all in such incredible heat, with the wagons still rolling onward to Ban Pong. We were literally up to our ankles in sewage, so to speak. Piled into these trucks with what possessions we still mercifully had, haversacks were used as seats embroiled in sewage too; odd garments were soon strung up to dry out from the sweaty environment we now found ourselves in. It looked truly pitiful inside these wagons, believe me... it was pitiful too.

We stopped for fuel and water and the locals would try to barter with us selling their wares. Local men carrying two baskets of fruit across their shoulders was a common sight by now, those who were fortunate enough to have some money left could buy fruit or eggs (cook cook or no cook) being cooked or raw eggs for sale, but these locals were soon swamped with starving hungry men begging from them for some food, and this was to be our lot twenty-four hours on end, for four long days and nights. It seemed like it might last for eternity... God forbid.

After another day or so in the stifling carriages we stopped to exchange engines or something. There was always the inevitable mad dash for the edge of the track for the necessary ablutions, no modesty now, out in the open, hardly any clothes, just the basic panic of nature taking its toll on men's bodies and no facilities or amenities for cleaning yourself down afterwards either.

One occasion when it was my turn to have my head out of the door, on one of the stops, lo and behold the engine backed on to the trucks but did not couple up to the chains and pipes properly. The engine puffed away and some of the trucks began to eventually roll on, but the train as a whole was not coupled up properly. I said to the lads in our carriage, "Don't panic. If the driver has any sense he'll let the trucks roll on and catch him and the engine up." Lots of the boys in the other trucks behind ours jumped out fearing a crash, the Japs went absolutely mad, firing over their heads into the air... what a sight to see all those boys maybe half a mile or more back on the line, cowering in the bushes then being herded once again at gun point back into their trucks. Luckily all the POWs with Juggy and myself remained calm, mainly due to many of them being so ill from dysentery anyway... we reckoned our three Jap guards nearly smoked themselves to death to kill the stench, as you see some chaps made it their duty to mess just inside the door and you can guess what it was like. The Japs really couldn't speak English but it was pretty plain what they were trying to say. What a state that poor old train and its trucks were left in but we just didn't care. Then our dignity had been drained and bashed out of us, I guess. A journey in my lifetime that I will never forget.

CHAPTER EIGHT

NOVEMBER/DECEMBER 1942

BUILDING THE RAILBED

After four days of so-called travelling in this mobile incarceration and as the train forced its way up into the hills, it stopped every so often to let off a certain number of POWs. Imagine how we all looked, filthy dirty, exhausted and stinking to high heaven.

Men were then set to making some kind of camp around this new area we found ourselves in. Bamboo and other materials were brought in by river ready to start building our own dwelling huts, which sadly were to become our wretched homes for use whilst preparing this railway of death... some holiday camp was to follow over the next months and years to come!

As the holiday train finally came to a halt and dropped off its remaining cargo of men, it stopped at Ban Pong deep in the jungles of Thailand. We were ordered off the train as this was the end of the line and then we trudged mile after mile on foot, many of us totally barefoot, having lost or worn out our shoes long beforehand. We plodded on ankle deep in sludge and filth, human excrement overflowing from camps already formed around the route we were trekking in, all of which had improper cess pits to take the amount of human waste. Then we carried on plodding through and deeper and deeper into dense jungle.

Occasionally a certain amount of men were dropped off from the trekking party to build a camp out of what they could find. I went on further with others, sleeping in the open when allowed to rest, dropping down and sleeping through sheer exhaustion. Until eventually I was dropped off at Chungkai with a party of men, this is where I spent nearly two and a half years

The first day we had to erect huts the best we could make from bamboo, banana leaves, palm fronds and foliage strips. Creepers from trees were attached to the structures, which acted as the strapping to tie everything tightly together. Leaving a space underneath the overhanging roof area and the side walls, to act as a window area where we would be able to see out from and watch what was going on in and around the camp. Then on the morrow just about six men were left to fully complete the huts, whilst others were taken down to start building the railway embankment.

This was our first encounter with what is now the infamous railway of death. We were now about to play our part in its creation.

Drawing chunkles, pick axes and spades, you name it... but still nothing mechanical not even a tractor, every single thing had to be done by hand. It was soon evident what the Japanese civil engineers wanted from us. Thousands of tons of soil had to be moved, trees had to be cut down and cut up into certain lengths and stacked in piles, roots dug out, and bamboo roots took some effort in shifting, I can tell you. Not to mention the felling of some enormous and beautiful hardwood trees.

All this labour was necessary for the rail bed to be made and laid ready for the embankment to be built up and all this time doing these tasks, the Japs were standing guard over you. Armed and holding anything they could use on you, such as a walking stick, iron bars, bamboo, pick axe handles. They pressured everyone into working from dawn until dark in all the elements the weather could muster. It was all right for them, they had a trench coat on to keep out the monsoon rains; we were now almost to a man practically naked except for the loin cloth.

The rail bed was ploughing on, winding and making its course through heavily forested areas, up hillsides and down into ravines, along the rivers edge and so it ploughed on relentlessly. Us working our fingers to the bones, no matter what the costs to human life or local countryside, always under the ever watchful eyes of our captors, eager to remind us of how swiftly we should be working. Whether they managed to lean up against a tree, or lie resting somewhere nearby it didn't take them a split second to spot anyone taking it a bit easier, that wasn't to be heard of. To slacken off in any way was inviting trouble; we learnt in the very early days that to fall behind or fail them in any way resulted only in punishment. They were swift to spot a weakness of any kind, they had the upper hand and they certainly never tired of using it. These were the mighty Japanese Imperial Army and we were their slaves in every sense of the word.

Intense heat the like of which we had not been accustomed to, stifling humidity, and even their monsoon rains. Men would sometimes start to sing to try to lift flagging spirits, but this was soon cut short usual by a hefty cuff around the head and a lot of shouting from the Japs. So all the noise that could usually be heard was that of the implements crashing into the hard surface beneath our bare feet, but there was a lot of uttering and swearing also going on from the prisoners being totally demoralised by our plight. Exhausted from the hard labour, starving hungry, desperately thirsty, trekking miles to and from our camp huts, climbing up and down the high embankment levels several feet high. Usually a mud slide down and an excruciating climb back up, moving earth and rubble to make way for the gangs behind us who would lay the sleepers and tracks for their railway to run along. I never actually laid any sleepers at all but worked with the earlier gangs, further forward up the lines preparing the surface and digging up roots and moving the earth and rocks, for this rail bed to be formed.

This work continued for about two months or so and our tasks were indeed heavy work, in places we were clambering up and down about 20 to 30 feet on the embankments and what made matters worse was the continual rain. All the trees and undergrowth had been felled so there was nothing to grasp hold of to help pull you up, so we were slipping and sliding all over the place.

The bags of soil were obviously heavier when so wet, by the time you had lugged great big boulders up and down those embankments slopes you knew about it, every muscle in your body ached.

You really felt the pain in your legs and arms to a point where it was almost impossible to move. It would always be at the point that a Jap guard would spot you had paused for breath or to wipe your brow and he, or they, would kick out with boots and lash out with their fists, or prod you fiercely with a stick, or whack you across your bare back with a bamboo cane.

The Japs soon realised that if they split open the ends of their bamboo canes, when they whacked it across your bare back it would whip together at the ends of the cane, nipping and rending your skin still deeper and cause further suffering, guaranteeing to tear the flesh on your back even more, and some of those bamboo canes would be better described as poles. Most of these guards had become evil and sadistic creatures of men, it didn't take them many months to perfect their cruel deeds and they could certainly dish out the pain and took great delight by constantly revelling in it... laughing in your face with a cynical grin from ear to ear. How we would have loved to retaliate not so much at your own punishment, but certainly when you saw other very ill men suffering such atrocities!

Bamboo certainly had its uses and it is almost too difficult to put the suffering into words. Sadly only those who found themselves there can really comprehend it. This was how we worked reloading the bags and shifting the soil and rocks, felling enormous trees for hours, days and weeks and into years on end.

With no real break allowed whatsoever except ten minutes twice a day for a cup of so-called tea, plus a half hour lunch stop for the rice rations. In the earlier times and obviously when we were working nearer to the cook house, we used to have the rice brought over to us, later and as we worked further away from our camp, we took our rice out with us in the morning, so you can guess by lunch time it had started to crawl on its own. Many of the men were incredibly ill by this time; the death rate was rising fast. We were forced to carry on until we had built up the embankment, for the railway to run upon, and so we carried on until we reached the mountainside at the foot of what must have been the Himalayan range.

Each night at dusk we were ordered back to our camp huts and had to be force marched under armed guard, but the longer we made the embankment and the railroad, the further we had to trudge back and forth, morning and night carrying all our tools back with us. Some tools slung over bamboo poles, others carried the best we could with the energy we had left after such an arduous day. In the evening it was a common sight to see men helping each other back due to sheer exhaustion, those who fell behind were prodded with sticks or abused in some way or other; for some I have no doubt that they would have been bayoneted or kicked to death by a Jap for falling behind anyway.

Those walks to and from the rail bed were indeed arduous treks to say the very least, but at least the homeward journey at night meant some food and some rest from our day's hard labour, and a time to catch up with the news of other men's events during the day.

It didn't end when we reached our camp. Then the guard counted back all the implements and God help anyone who had lost something or damaged anything; this along with body searches. If a POW had been lucky enough to scrounge an egg from a local native en route, this having been quickly hidden under someone's hat would soon be smashed and running down his face, as the Japs soon found out about this little extra food that was to help someone's meagre ration go just that little bit further. I recall sugar being brought back into camp in water dixies and slung onto bamboo poles the POWs used to swing the dixies, pretending as though it were empty to elude the eyes of the ever wary Japs.

Butter, believe it or not, was used to grease up the Japs' vehicles and ammunition, so needless to say several ounces of that was stowed away under the precious few hats that remained and made it back to the cook house... if the POW was lucky to trick the guards.

Another thing that used to help us out was, POWs were given the task of cleaning out the Jap living quarters and if a half-used bottle of ointment lay around that soon went walkabouts and back for one of our poor souls to make good use of, but I hasten to add that all of these extras were indeed a rarity.

We would bathe in the river the best we could at night, given how tired we were, then be given our evening meagre ration of rice. Afterwards we were paraded (tenco) and everybody, even the sick and stretcher cases had to be lined up, and counted per hut. The NCO would count us all off and report the numbers to the Japs.

We thought that the railway we were building would skirt around the mountainside we had reached but no... the day came when hundreds of men, a percentage of those who had been building the embankment, had to draw a 14lb hammer and a 2 foot iron chisel. Being ordered off to work in pairs, each pair then went off. I was one of such a pair of men.

We clambered and climbed just over halfway up the mountainside and there we began hammering and chiselling away. One man holding the chisel steady, whilst the other man banged away with the hammer for all his might, until we had knocked or effectively drilled a hole I believe about 5 inches deep. We then stood back and the Japs put dynamite into the holes and blew the rock face to pieces. This work took ages to complete. We used to hit the chisel in pairs almost like formation workers, hitting and twisting the chisel into the rock floor until the hole was deep enough, so that the rock face could be blown apart to start breaking the mountainside apart, hence forming the cutting.

Our hands would be skin bare, raw weeping flesh; blisters didn't have time to form on your skin, it was down to raw flesh on your hands in no time flat. As we hammered and chiselled away, up would come another gang and they collected all the pieces of rock and duly carried out all the fragments clear of the cutting we were forging.

The POWs were still all of one mind to work as slowly as they could humanly get away with, trying to hamper progress of the line by reducing our work speed wherever possible, but the ever watchful guards were always hovering above us, hitting out or pelting us with rocks and stones if we slowed down. We did ourselves no favours and the last thing we felt like was doing them a favour by completing this railway task. Alas our actions encouraged our captors to give us men many more ear bashings.

Other men had been sent around the mountainside and were hard at work carrying on with the embankment from where our cutting was being made down through the rock's surface. My word, our poor hands they were totally skin bare. We almost prayed for a tin of Germolene but nothing was given to us by way of ointment, bandages or treatment at all, just "Speedo" and bash after bash. "Pinto presento" was very prevalent that was a hard slap around the face by any guard when he felt fit to do so.

We eventually got through that mountain rock down to where the level of the railway was to be laid. The gap, or Chungkai Cutting as it was to be called, that we had exposed, was approximately 50 feet deep by about 20 feet wide and ran some 200 yards or more in length. All of that rock being removed by human hand; sadly many men died from exhaustion, starvation, dysentery, malaria etc... having been brought out from their sick beds and made to work on, alongside us gangs of men, no matter how sick they were. Those terribly ill would be set to work breaking up stones just to keep them busy, given a trivial task that didn't really need doing, but this was a form of punishment from the Japs for being ill in the first place. They showed no mercy whatsoever to anyone. It didn't matter to the Japs.

Some men just passed out and lay and died where they were. We just buried many where they fell, not being allowed to carry them back at night to the camp cemetery. Japs literally forced us to bury men, our colleagues, in the embankment itself where we were working, so how on earth exact numbers could be accounted for at the end of the war defeats me, as there were no visible bamboo crosses for those sad victims.

SOLID ROCK CUTTING

Once the cutting was almost complete the Japs brought up three light trucks but no engine. Victor Bowers (Canning Town, London) was put in charge of men pushing those trucks loaded with the rubble from our labour and he then had to catch up a gang further up the line where the rubble was to be used to set up the rail bed embankment.

It was on a Monday on an empty return journey with those trucks that Victor was singing, "Once I've built a railway and made it run against time." A famous song in its day. All hell broke loose again. Up jumped a Jap and smashed Victor on his legs, beating him several times with the butt of his weapon. How the demented Jap didn't break his bones to smithereens I just don't know and all because the Jap didn't like him singing. How terribly sad things were.

Oh! What a do... it was like living in a so-called hell, but with the Lord's help I managed to come through that ordeal.

It was all too clear that these Japanese soldiers, and indeed their Korean counterparts who were just as bad, simply hated the sight of us Brits and others too. We were scum, nothing in their eyes but hated slaves, and back then we hated them too!

There could be no reprisal or uprising for that would have meant certain death. A very cheap labour force indeed, many of us men were beaten extremely cruelly and harshly at regular intervals, the most savage of brutality sometimes for the sheer fun of it. If anyone died their attitude was it was one less mouth to feed and so the hatred on both sides intensified but it drove you on to hopefully come through this ordeal alive.

The weather was either scorching hot and we were given very little water to drink, or on the other hand we had to endure torrential downpours. Whatever the elements, we worked on relentlessly. Their monsoons lasted for about four weeks on end, relentless heavy stair rods of rain, rivers would quickly rise and flood the area, making sanitation even more perilous. Local kampongs, housing for the natives, could be seen floating down the river as homes were washed away in the flood waters, but we were forced to work on only to return at night to a flooded hut to try to rest the best we could; it was sheer purgatory.

Whilst working in Chungkai, at our so-called holiday camp in this heart-breaking jungle, which was to be our destination and my home eventually for more than three and a half long and weary years, my heart was so broken I hardly had the strength to plod on, but plod on I did, not daring to think of home, Joyce, my parents, brothers and sisters or anything else other than sheer survival. It sounds selfish now but it was every man for himself if he wanted to come through alive. It was at this point, January 1943, that the pace really hotted up with the so-called Jap "Speedo" campaign. Everything had to be done even faster, perhaps down to our own fault for not complying with this "Speedo" campaign earlier. The Japs would grab the hammers and implements out of our hands, give us a hefty clout around the ears and then show us how to work faster. The length of the working day increased significantly too, with the Japs constantly reminding us that we had a deadline to meet and they made jolly sure we kept to their targets from then on in.

The death rate was rising fast with this added pressure, our ever diminishing strength meant we were less effective in our labour at building their rail bed and those rendered useless by this pressure only brought on more beatings for themselves and for many... death. We were now a totally expendable force in their eyes, useless and no good to man nor beast. It seemed like years ago that we buried our first POW. He had a coffin and was the only one to be afforded such a burial. This coffin was considered too costly, so from then on men were buried in their own blankets if they had one, stitched up at the sides.

The locals were also suffering great hardship and what they used to do was to watch the funeral services take place, memorise the latest burial ground and go back under the cover of darkness, dig up our comrades and pinch their blankets, reburying the bodies as they went. This was noticed by our officers, in that the burial grounds had been disturbed and once their scam had been rumbled, men were from then on buried in rice sacks.

It was also common for a service to be stopped for one man and before he was buried, a second body would accompany him. As I said the death rate was alarming. Many occasions sights would leave you staring, speechless in disbelief at what was unfolding around you.

Colonel Johnson stood up at one time and clearly told us all point blank that only those with the strongest willpower will stand any chance of pulling through this awful predicament. It was now just hell on earth, starvation, ill treatment, with hardly any food other than a handful of rice and "Speedo", "Speedo" bellowed at you all the day long. I could go on for a very long period of time, talking about the incidents that I witnessed happening, men having to stand for hours on end, holding either heavy rocks above their heads whilst standing in the boiling sun, or being tied down and having water poured down their nostrils hence flooding their lungs. Men jumped upon and squashed to their inevitable deaths. Many men beaten so severely that their bones broke very easily, that's just to name but a few of the types of punishment dished out to the POWs. The sights were horrendous, we could do nothing to stop these endless barbaric atrocities taking place, we could just be there for the victim, tend to him after his punishment ended and support him, should he be lucky enough to survive the onslaughts.

Having been in the jungle for several months I recall back at camp how I was knocked out unconscious by a Jap with a pick axe handle. He caught me right behind my ear. It happened because he demanded that a party of about 60 men who were bathing in the river should come out of the water immediately. Being me I ordered all the men out, had them line up and counted and reported the number to the Jap in charge of us. I still couldn't understand his language properly nor he mine, where upon he just hit me as hard as he possibly could. Out I went for the count, unknowingly rolled down the embankment towards the river, a drop of some 30 to 40 feet where upon my mates broke rank and clambered down and dragged me back out. Without their prompt action I would have perished to my death or been eaten by a crocodile no doubt. An interpreter was fetched and he soon explained to the Jap that I had done what he had ordered, but what we didn't realise was, that some men had broken out of the rear of the rank and scampered into the jungle for fear that they too would take such a beating. Here incidentally, maybe I should add, we were paid the princely sum of approximately one dollar a week for our labour, which was paid out via our own officers.

Escapement was impossible, there would be about 200

POWs and about 50 heavily armed Japs working in a close party. You might think why not overcome them and make your escape, not so easy with frailty and sickness beyond belief, it made any thoughts of escape quickly disappear from your mind… They were heavily armed and fit men with machine guns, rifles, even bamboo poles and iron bars and wouldn't think twice about using them or shooting an escapee in the back. Some prisoners did make an attempt to escape and were quickly caught; those who weren't physically kicked to death by the Japs were tortured to death by some other wicked deed, and in the full view of our eyes too. Their way of warning others not to try escaping! So you can see no one really contemplated the idea, there was jungle itself to get through, food and water would be needed, transportation, none of which were at our disposal. Anyway, where could we lay our hands freely upon such things, so how could we escape, how would we survive, where would we go even if we did make a break for it; you would have to be completely mad to have dared to risk escaping. The jungle alone would have claimed its own victims, let alone those Japs chasing after you!

I have to say towards the end of our captivity it was on my mind and those of my friends to make a break for it. Had the war not ended when it did, who knows, I might not have been here now to relay my side of the story!!

CHAPTER NINE

BAMBOO

This thriving vegetation grew absolutely everywhere. It was quite colourful on its own. Black stems of bamboo through to various green shaded stems. Canes that were just a few feet high, with little shoots attached, would, almost overnight, grow to be some eight to ten feet tall. It grew like wildfire, was very prolific and soon formed some huge clumps, all growing away merrily only for us to come along and uproot it

This was stubborn vegetation to shift and took some intense labour to remove all the roots and shoots from one clump alone. The jungle floor was littered with bamboos of every shape and size, so many man hours were spent in dealing with this invasive shrub. You could eat some of the younger parts of the plant but now we readily eat bamboo shoots, by the tons I suspect. We didn't really know that at the time when we were almost imprisoned by it, worked hard with it and learnt to use it to its fullest potential in many life-saving ways.

If bamboo was growing were the Japs wanted to build the railway line then it was felled. Much of the bamboo was sawn down. Larger bamboo canes, or rather poles of about 8 to 10 inches across and several feet long, was floated down the River Kwai to the sawmills and used for their war efforts.

Bamboo had its many, many uses. The larger pieces some twenty foot high and at least sixteen inches across were used to erect our huts and sleeping quarters. Our beds were made of bamboo slats and pretty uncomfortable at that for as many years as we had to endure them. Operating tables and rough chairs for the medical room were made from poles of bamboo. Bamboo served its purpose in the hospital areas as effective bed pans. Also cups were formed by cutting just above the joint of the bamboo and served us as effective substitutes for our drinking vessel.

A lot of bamboo was used for the cook house fires, to heat up our rice mush. A great deal of the bamboo was cut into lengths and neatly piled ready at the sides of the embankments for the railway engines, to use later, no doubt. Amputees were grateful for their bamboo crutches or even replacement limbs, legs especially, which remarkably, some clever men had the vision and ability to create and craft. Once received by the victim they changed a man's appearance and attitude to life in a matter of minutes. It was used in abundance at the latrines, even the funeral piers were erected of this material and indeed to the humble cross itself for the many sad and unfortunate victims that this war was claiming. Our cemeteries were becoming crammed with bamboo crosses.

Later on towards the end of the war in Konkuita, about a dozen men formed felling parties and were specifically ordered to go out and cut so much bamboo a day, along with other hardwood of any type, cutting it into certain metre lengths and creating so high and so long a stack of logs. I worked on one such party after leaving the police at Chungkai.

After returning home and with a family of my own to raise I used the bamboo canes time and time again in my own garden. One fond memory being that of growing my sweet peas against the bamboo canes. Needless to say even in my own back garden my heartfelt thoughts would go back to the jungle and my days of captivity. Harrowing scenes the likes of which we witnessed as POWs will never, never fade and hence this book bears the humble cross and reminders of the bamboo on its cover.

CHAPTER TEN

FEBRUARY/MARCH 1943

MY TIME IN THE POLICE FORCE AT CHUNGKAI/THAILAND

Time was rolling on but it was increasingly difficult to keep track of the days and indeed the time of day. We had few wrist watches left between us, no diaries and no calendars to refer to. Above all we had no news of any kind, either how the war was progressing or more importantly from home. Not a letter or postcard to cling to, we simply had no idea whatsoever as to what was going on in the outside world. We had effectively, very effectively, been cut off from civilisation, and for years successfully cut off from our own country and people. A forgotten force of men not hearing anything through the thickness of the jungle and being hundreds and hundreds of miles from anywhere, so to speak. Could we be here for ever, I wondered!

The Dear Lord looked after me wonderfully in so much that I was asked to join the camp police and spent the last year and a half as a military policeman joining up with some twenty other policemen. Much to the dislike of some POWs but the appreciation of my real mates. It turned out to be the best day's work my officers did for me; they basically saved my life from here on in so to speak.

Losing my watch all those months earlier was not to be my only prized possession I was to loose, or have stolen from me. My wallet complete with contents, photographs and what precious little money I had also soon disappeared. Miraculously a few months later my officer called me over and asked if I knew the person on the photograph. I beamed. I should think I did; it was Joyce my fiancée.

FIANCÉE JOYCE

This picture of my fiancée Joyce accompanied me throughout my captivity from there on. So now at least something beautiful to hold on dearly to, as for the rest of the stolen gear... well who knows. Thieving was beginning to become some men's favourite pastime, as anything they could steal could then be used to barter for food or cigarettes later on. I still have that photograph of Joyce proudly on display today.

I gladly didn't have to go out with the working parties in the morning to build the rail bed, although strangely I was left feeling sad as the sight of the columns of men as they trudged away at dawn. Their weary heels kicking up a dust storm as they tramped away, still tired and forlorn even before their days hard toiling began further up the line. I stayed back at camp to do the police duties that were assigned to me.

With hundreds and hundreds of POWs moving relentlessly back and forth, in and out and through the camps, many arriving from having worked further behind us, back down the line, their work back there now completed, they would then camp with us but were soon drafted out and joined other gangs that would progressively move out and on; they went further upland. Men were constantly on the move keeping pace with the line itself.

With the sick men in their hospitals and still some poor wretched souls locked up in their pitiful coolers at all times of the day and night, our work was still well and truly cut out. Being a policeman wasn't easy. It gave you no privileges and we received little or no mercy from the Japs even as policemen. Remember they had no respect for law and order, only their own type of course.

We had plenty of guard duty to keep us occupied in the police force, ensuring there was no excessive noise going on, no fires being lit, no POWs trying to escape and no fighting over food. If we heard any disturbances from the hospital wards, then it was our duty to run over to assist or call a medical officer to attend, I witnessed many harrowing scenes in just that duty alone and felt so incredibly sorry for the many men afflicted by whatever illness had laid hold of them.

I did rejoin the gangs on the working parties some eighteen months later when I left Chungkai, but more of that when I mention Konkuita, the dreaded Konkuita!

I was moved from the working party huts to the military police hut, which then became my home and accommodation from then on in. I was made up to a sergeant but the War Office never acknowledged this as it wasn't published on battalion orders, no surprises there... in other words the officer in charge never put it on paper to nail to the tree as we had no paper. Then again, all the trees nearby had been felled. Never mind, it didn't alter the way I felt or how I carried out my duties as a policeman. I still strangely felt a privileged man and gave of my very best.

I believe I did a great work for the police there as thieving was rampant albeit most of it petty thieving, but it would cause a huge ruckus nevertheless. There were many men apprehended for one so-called crime or another. I caught a man selling a blanket to the Thai folk. Local natives, who were ready and willing to give ten dollars of Thai money for a blanket, watches, anything saleable was stolen and sold over the fence. You can guess my luck, when I went back to my bed space one night my blanket had gone too, but my best mate Mort said, "Don't worry, Sid, bring a knife" and we proceeded to halve his blanket, so we both finished up with half a blanket each.

That's what you call real comradeship. During such atrocities, with every man thinking only of his own survival, Victor was still willing to share his blanket with me. Even half a blanket could prove life-saving from the many bugs that would attach themselves to your flesh overnight. One bite alone would leave you with a very nasty bout of malaria in the bargain.

During my time with the police I was ordered to reflect a mirror onto the operating tables whilst the medical officers carried out major surgery such as amputating the boys' legs due to tropical ulcers. Terrible, terrible sights to be involved with, seeing these men's limbs cut away, watching their bodies writhing in pain and all limbs removed with no anaesthetic at all, men gallantly enduring indescribable pain; despite the bravery their screams could be deafening. All operations would be carried out in our so-called hospital operating theatre. Some form of receptacle would be bubbling away on the side to sterilise the crude surgical implements, the odd bin would be there to collect any debris from the operation procedure. There were no such things as surgically clean gowns and rubber gloves, just the bare hands of dedicated and skilful medical officers. All truly great men willing to help their comrades in distress, men to whom many of us owe such an enormous debt of thanks.

As I would stand holding a mirror, catching the sun beam on it and thereby creating extra shafts of light, by reflecting it down onto the operating bed for the surgeon to carry out his procedure, so another POW would wait to take away the severed limb and bury it, whilst someone else would be helping pass up the implements needed for completing the surgery. There would be one or two of these surgery days every three to four weeks; much needed they were too. Pluckier men would try their luck in the meanwhile in the river, bathing whilst the sticklebacks ate at their ulcers, sores or other infections, clearing away the pus and infection from their wounds. Not a pleasant thing to do but preferable to the pain of amputation...

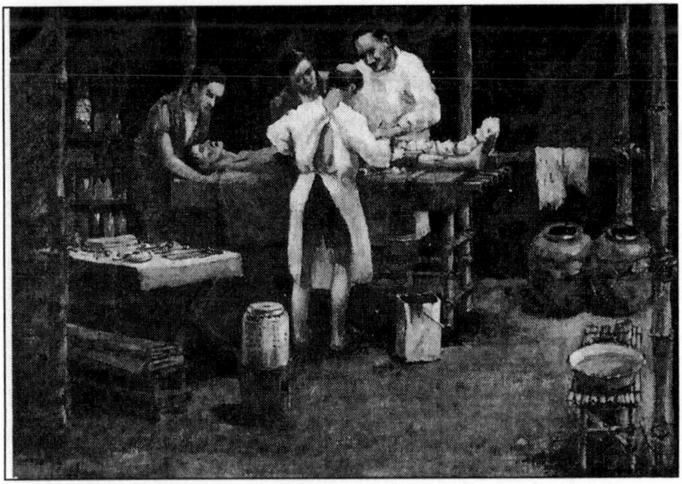

HOSPITAL OPERATING THEATRE
CHUNGKAI

So many men were going down with ulcers the medical officers had no alternative but to say to those afflicted "You either let me operate or you can have a rice sack," in other words face death and be buried in a rice sack. Some sadly chose the latter, too fearful of the operation procedure, having doubtlessly witnessed and heard the screams from the operating table. That piercing yell alone was enough to put off even the sturdiest and hardest of all men.

After the medical officer had finished the operation procedure, Major Moon would come to me and say, "Lockwood, you know what to do" and I would take a twenty minute break, then report back for duty again. I helped whilst five men had amputations in one day, scenes I just cannot forget. Col. Dunlop was the main medical officer but he has now sadly passed away. Major Moon was another fine man. Both were Australians and life savers in the truest sense of the word; many more men would have perished without their dedicated skill and care.

Prisoners' skills soon came to the fore as a result of all this surgery, with several men being able to make artificial limbs of some kind or other, using vegetation and bamboo from the jungle. Mainly bamboo and creepers, or by scrounging or even pinching what they could, from where they could, to make some form of aid for the amputees. Most of these stricken men still remained cheerful once they healed from their ordeal, hobbling around on their crutches, sitting chatting to one another trying to keep up their spirits, for them, most of them anyway, their war could have been considered well and truly over, but not so. The Japanese gave them no respite and they were ordered like the rest, to continue with the working parties. So, crippled as they were, they too joined in the ranks of men working on the lines breaking up stones. This must have been where the saying "Keep going the spirit that kept us going" sprang up from. These men were an inspiration to us all for sure.

Sadly, despite the doctors' heroic actions, many men were dying from various illnesses and starvation and I witnessed up to nineteen funerals in one day. It was my task to make all the men around stand to attention allowing the burial parties to proceed, many having to be bellowed at to stand still, as they were past caring so to speak, due to ill health of their own to contend with and the fact that death was a constant and relentless companion.

Over 3000 men were buried at Chungkai alone and graveyards were springing up all around us. Chungkai was just one of the many camps that I alone found myself in during the war. A picture is shown at the end of this chapter of a War Cemetery as it stands today, peaceful and beautiful now, but a far cry from the rugged bamboo crosses with no name tags during our days as POWs.

During this stay with the police, it was in this camp that I saw what I thought to be a member of the fifth columnist. He was a black man, strong and fine at about six foot tall. He just stared at you in such a way that you dare hardly breathe let alone speak. I have to say I felt scared stiff of him but then again, what did he think of us staring back like wild men, thin and gaunt from our ill treatment and starvation, eyes sunken back into predominant cheek bones, flesh blackened by the weather, bodies scarred by our captors? At another reunion dinner after the war ended, one of our officers confided in me that a Thai man found him out in the camp and gave him a considerable amount of money. Where it came from was a mystery. It was believed to have come through the fifth columnist movement, probably brought in through the very man I have mentioned, but then again is my imagination running wild now, it hasn't so far, but who knows, who were these men, how many were there in our midst that we were totally oblivious to?

I recall whilst at Chungkai, we built one of the huts as and when we had the time, between working shifts so to speak, when I recall seeing a linen line dangling from our hut over to the nearby tree. Me being Joe Muggins, I truly thought this was a washing line, but then again with hindsight, what washing, the odd tangled and bedraggled bandage, the odd jock strap of a loin cloth, perhaps I should have thought better of it at the time, having but a handful of so-called clothing between us. I should have been sharper on the uptake but I wasn't. At that time the officers were still sharing huts with us, they used the beds just inside the doorway. After that period of time, many were mysteriously taken away and several ill treated according to later accounts.

What I was told after the war was, that linen line turned out to be wire used for the illegal wireless that was stowed in our very hut. Little did I know. I never saw it being used and was totally unaware of the radio's existence at the time. At one of our FEPOW reunion meetings after the war, it was confirmed to me on very reliable authority that there were in fact two wirelesses operating from our sleeping quarters. My nights would have been somewhat even more fragmented had I known of the terrible risk our officers were taking, right in our midst and under our very noses. The truth of the matter is that one officer would sit outside the hut, pretending to be reading his book. The slightest movement he detected would be motioned back inside the hut to the officers attempting to gain their news snippets over the airwaves. Such was the quietness and stealth of their operation, what bravery too, as to be caught would have meant certain beheading, death for those officers and presumably for us POWs sharing the huts as well, as no amount of pleading would have convinced the Japs that we were oblivious to such actions.

It transpired that these wirelesses were kept inside the main bamboo poles, the very poles which held the roof of our hut up. A main segment of the pole was skilfully carved out of the upright so that it didn't show to anyone. The whole section removed to get to the apparatus, perform the illegal deed, glean as much information as at all possible in a short period of time, then stow the wireless quickly away at the sight or sound of a Jap. What nerve and bravery!

At the end of the war when the release happened apparently the wirelesses must have surfaced from all around and from goodness knows where. The Japs couldn't touch them of course by this stage. It was about three days after we knew of the war ending that even some Australians asked me to go and see their set, calling me over to where they sat and said, "Hullo, Sheila, come and see this wireless man, have a beer and listen to the news from home." It was actually Rangoon talking to the prisoners, so I know of that very existence, but apparently the Japs asked our officers how they smuggled the wireless from camp to camp. The funny end to this tale is, it was smuggled out in the Japs' belongings, as our men had to carry their gear further up the line of course, and those in charge of this contraband rightly felt, the last place the Japs would check would be their own luggage and baggage. So they whipped the wireless equipment into the Japs' own gear without them noticing... one up to the POWs and their officers eh!

Bill Procter about whom I shall share another funny story with you later on in the book, was the man who could get his hands on just about anything and everything. Ducking and diving under the fences at all hours of the day and night, and so he was able to get out to his native contacts and arrange most things. Spare parts for the wireless being one precious gift that he could easily secure. So his true grit and determination helped in a way I hadn't realised at the time.

Amongst other duties I also recall turning away about fifteen or so Tamils, both men and women plus various other nationals, from our camp entrance, as the Japs had strictly ordered us not to allow anyone else in case they carried cholera. So we had to stand our ground and move these poor beleaguered folk on. They were just skin over bone, pleading eyes, shabby skeletons having been forced to work elsewhere in the jungle and had been abandoned and left to their own fate, not needed because of their ill health and inability to work, having already been worked virtually to death elsewhere anyway. As they tramped away past our site it was obvious to me, that those poor skeletons of men, dressed merely in rags, would certainly soon be dead. It was as if they had already had it in life and felt and looked completely finished. They swore and cursed at us as they went on past but there was nothing anyone could do, our camp was already in a pretty run down dilapidated state. So they wandered on into oblivion, just a few handful of human beings, whose numbers were so relatively few, that their numbers wouldn't even have mattered inside our pitiful camp. Such was the determination of the Japs; they had to go on past. That was all the Japs cared about anyone's life in general, except of course their own. After the war finished it soon became all too apparent just how many of these nationals had in fact perished at the hands of the Japs. They died in their many thousands and thousands.

It was during my work as a policeman that I realised I was now much more fortunate than some of my fellows. I had a little more freedom which I had to use wisely, you understand, I wasn't about to take advantage and be a dead hero. It was hard enough to survive and exist without inviting a bashing, so stepping outside of the camp perimeter for us on duty was allowed, as long as we didn't stray too far afield. This little taste of freedom went on for about six months, no longer.

It was on times like this that POWs would ask us to try and sell their bits and pieces outside of the camp to raise a few pennies so to speak. It was bits and pieces too. Even officers would give us say maybe their watch to sell on to the locals to raise money or to exchange for a morsel of food. Sometimes though, the locals would take offence at our actions and would turn against us for what appeared no real reason, so you bided your time, stayed well clear and tried again another day. If you met up with their animosity you just quietly, but quickly, slid back into camp, not wishing to draw attention to our bartering skills outside of the camp.

One night my mate Don Dawson had left such a fracas behind him and returned with me to camp, only to get itchy feet a while later and then he decided to try his luck again really quickly. He was successful, but alas only in getting one almighty hiding from the locals. Such was the high risk of our doings that he effectively went missing and we didn't see him for a few hours. Needless to say I was worried sick about Don knowing roughly where he would have been when he went missing, but it would have been folly to attempt to go to find him and try to rescue him.

Don, worse still, was still missing from our daily tenco roll call that evening, so someone had to stand in for him, moving up in the ranks as the counting was effectively taking place under the eyes of the not so wary Japs. So you can see how quickly things could go completely wrong, and our daredevil exploits soon involved other mates, putting their lives on the line. But do remember we were all desperate and hungry men. We would do anything to get at some food or money to buy wares from locals if we possibly could and get it back to the camp by any means possible. It was out on such so-called adventures that I saw heaps and heaps of peanuts, piled high on rush matting to dry in the sun. If we knew the local man involved we might be lucky to be given a few, just four or five peanuts, nothing more. Hardly a mouthful but an extremely welcome change to rice scratchings.

I saw a few Buddha temples out in the jungle clearings, not friendly places to be, but ideal for our selling ground. I must say I found them to be quite intimidating and frightening buildings at the time, but then again at the time I counted it as a privilege being in the police force as this enabled me to see a little more of what was on the outside of those camp fences.

WAR CEMETERY

CHAPTER ELEVEN

MID 1943

SAMMY AND MR BULL

My possessions were extremely limited but my dixie and spoon miraculously moved with me up to Thailand. There the natives used to try to sell us a pasta-like dish called marmee, something I have never found since and possibly haven't even spelt correctly today. The natives used to move on to the edge of our camps and run a little type of canteen and if anybody had got enough money left, they could purchase their delights of hot marmee. I was fortunate on two or three of these occasions but it was a rarity actually, albeit a very welcome change from the blandness of rice itself.

I guess as time went on we had been prisoners for about a year and a half, when the rice situation had really worsened. Believe me it was bad enough to start with, now it was filthy dirty before it was cooked and try as they might that cooking process didn't do much to enhance it anyway. It was a common sight to see the POWs queue up for their meagre rations, squat down on the ground and proceed to flick the fat and juicy maggots out of their dixie with a spoon before they could eat their so-called meal. Yes seriously, if you were lucky you got an extra maggot or two to land in your own dixie. Whilst still in Chungkai and some six months later, maggot flicking had to cease. The officers said, "You can stop that game" and advised us to stop chucking them on the ground but to eat them and be grateful for the extra nourishment and also to slow down in how fast we were gobbling down our rations anyway.

Can you envisage the scene? Overworked, skeleton-like, starving men gulping down their rice and rejoining the back of the queue for what would be a second helping. They'd do anything to get seconds; these were desperately hungry, no... starving, pathetic creatures of men. The boys would then also go through the huts and if anyone lay sick, too sick to eat their rice and too ill to answer, they would have their rice as well and quickly make short work of it. If the sick man hadn't been up for rice at all, they would take his dixie and draw his portion anyway and if someone had just died in the hut, well his rations were soon accounted for. Men even wearily crawling on their hands and knees back to their huts, on all fours with a mug of rice for sustenance. It was really a very pitiful sight to witness for us all, but by now we had lost many hundreds of comrades due to starvation alone, so we just had to eat what we had on offer.

I never knowingly ate snake or rat but if maggots were on the menu, then my guess is, if the cooks could, they would whip either of those creatures into us as well to aid our disastrous diet. Comrades since returning home have confirmed rats were eaten as commonplace and I have no reason to doubt their stories.

I came in contact with a man called Mr Bull whilst in the police at Chungkai and made friends with him and his family whilst on one of my walkabouts. He was about forty years of age and lived in a little kampong with his family about half a mile out from our camp. We met by chance just outside the camp perimeter and Mr Bull was a man who would always be trying to sell us something or other, or trying to bring something into camp for us POWs but he couldn't speak our language.

Sammy, his eight-year-old son, would come along to the camp with him. The Japs would allow the lad into the camp to mix with us and have a look around in general, nothing really being asked of him. Naturally, like all little boys of his age, he would wander around and play around at will, or wherever he could. Over the course of time he became quite at ease with us POWs and would always come and speak to me in particular and my group of close mates. Actually, we looked forward to his visits.

We taught Sammy to speak some English and he in turn helped us with some of his Thai language, so we began to get along together quite nicely, looking forward to a visit from this cheery little boy.

His father, well he was quite a big man and not easily missed. He appeared at the camp gate one day with two baskets of meat intended for us prisoners. So the Japs let him through with it; he got about one hundred yards into the camp when they stopped him. They took all his meat off him and took it to the Jap cook house. Then the four or five Japs turned their attention on him and began to savagely beat him. I witnessed them beating him unmercifully. I thought they would kill him there and then... but they didn't. Japs had perfected the knack of leaving a victim just before he was killed and intervening was unthought-of; it was more than we dared to do. We were trying to stay alive and survive this war somehow ourselves, but even sadder than our lack of intervention in this dreadful affray was that little Sammy witnessed his father's beating for himself. Can you image what he must have thought?

They left Mr Bull lying there for some time and in the end ordered somebody to throw a pail of water over him. This was always their antidote to a severe bashing. He eventually recovered, got up and went hobbling out of the camp with his young son helping him along to return to his family.

Poor man, lo and behold he returned a month later and did exactly the same thing again. Once again he came up to the camp gates with all this meat. Here we go again; they let him in, took the meat away from him and then severely set about him yet again. You would have thought the poor man would have realised what risk he was running but perhaps he wasn't quite sensible enough, or knowledgeable about life on the line, to comprehend what was happening to us inside the camp itself.

As a result of these two terrible happenings, Mr Bull suffering such intolerable beatings on our behalf, we got hold of his son Sammy and told him not to allow his father to return under any circumstances and take this risk again. We appreciated what he was trying to do for us and that he realised we were starving hungry, but he wasn't to risk his life anymore

Being a policeman I was allowed out of camp and I used to walk around by his kampong. Sometimes this could be a daily occurrence. I was able have a quick word or two with him in my broken Thai language. Mr Bull's home was pitiful really, nothing but a meagre shack and he had three children to raise. I saw the odd chicken or two scuttling around the place but as for livestock, what he must have done was to buy a bullock, or acquired it from someone to slaughter for us men. Hence the baskets of meat. What lengths this man and his family had gone to in an effort to help foreigners in his land.

It didn't end there. A few months later, the next thing we knew was Mr Bull had ventured to the camp gates yet again but this time with a live bullock. He opened the gate, slapped its back and let it loose to run into the camp. Of course you can imagine the mayhem that ensued. The bullock was downed within seconds, its throat was quickly cut, the beast slaughtered and cut into pieces before the Japs could get a handle on the situation. I would suggest it was in the pot before Mr Bull got back to his home. Now he had at last cottoned on to what fate awaited him but he avoided a third beating by his gallant actions this time. We fed all the better that evening because of his heroic deeds.

This might sound strange but the Japs wouldn't kill an animal or a snake, anything living like that, but they wouldn't think twice about killing a human being, especially us lot.

Mr Bull didn't return to camp again but I was privileged and able to go and see him from time to time. We could make basic communication, enough for him to say "Boom, boom Singapore or boom, boom Bangkok". He used to try to tell me something about Germany or Russia, in his way telling me what news he had been able to glean and naturally on return to camp I relayed this to my officers for them to make of it what they would. It was Mr Bull who relayed that bombs were dropping on the end of the line we had started building at Ban Pong. So gradually things were pieced together that some form of Allied attack and advance was happening, but how long would they take to reach us, how long could we hold out for, lots of questions and still no answers.

Whilst visiting Mr Bull at his home, usually and luckily enough for me, he would offer me a spoon full of rice on a banana leaf. Sometimes he'd give me a Red Bull cigarette, which is how we named him Mr Bull. Maybe he'd offer a tiny tot of his home made saki whisky. Mind you, not that the Japs were aware of my activity or whereabouts at the time, perish the thought. Having said that, I did get caught out of camp one afternoon just after the orders had been issued that anyone found outside the camp gates at night would be shot. Here we go again, along with a man called Kirby we were the first ones to be caught out of camp.

Jap guard Moonface was alone that afternoon when we were caught outside the camp gate and he spared Kirby and me from death. Moonface and Osour were the two commanding Jap guards that I had to face for this violation at Chungkai and if it had been left to Osour alone he would have gloried in it, rubbed his hands together and jumped for joy. I would for sure have been shot in the morning. Usually executions were performed outside of camp; I didn't personally witness such atrocity but knew of it happening. These two particular guards would stop at nothing, which was now very apparent; Moonface was the younger of the two men at about 30 years of age, towering above me at around 6 feet 3 inches. Osour was the older of the two and much shorter but still a defiant creature of a man to have close encounters with.

It wasn't the first encounter I had unfortunately had with Osour. He had caught me going into the church some time earlier on. I'd had several clips around the ear from that man. Some because I wasn't quick enough to bow properly when I met up with him, or salute him quickly enough. Any excuse was good enough for this man to bash me and I'm afraid I got to know him a little too well and he me. I should let you know that whilst in camp we had to bow and salute each time we met or passed a Jap guard. It wasn't quite so whilst you were working on the line as they were guarding us.

Osour would walk through the camps repeatedly and intentionally to make the boys salute and bow to him on purpose. He wallowed in his power. If we were too far away to realise it was him, he would call you over and "Pinto presento", another hard wallop around the ears. In the end we had to thank him for this treatment and if you didn't say thank you, well you can guess the rest can't you, another hard bashing and so it went on.

Anyway back to Mr Bull; he had precious little in life to give but even that he was willing to share with us boys. What he had got the Japs took, and it wasn't until later on in captivity and at the end of the war that I saw this remarkable old man yet again.

CHAPTER TWELVE

SPRING 1944

ONE OF MANY ILLNESSES

I'll start off this chapter by saying that if you had toothache the "dentist" would pull the offending tooth out with a pair of pliers and I know first hand of men having fillings made from raw cement!!

BERI BERI

Beri beri is caused by a severe lack of vitamin B. Wet Beri beri caused men's stomachs to swell up like some expectant woman; also necks and faces swelled beyond recognition. Some survived this illness but many men lost their lives to wet beri beri; many deformities were appearing on men's bodies.

Dry beri beri was less severe, nevertheless painful, causing aching in the bones and particularly the calves of your legs. So from your feet up to the knee could become very painful and restless. This was due again to lack of vitamins in our diet but you had to learn to live with it and unfortunately men still suffer from these symptoms and many other associated aliments today.

STRONGELOIDS

Parasites would enter through your skin, mainly the soles of your feet and remained in your body for years and years, so many of us know to our cost nowadays.

At the time of captivity you were unaware of these parasites and it wasn't until after the war ended that many of us had full medicals and were tested for these little blighters. Some men even underwent stomach operations in order to trace these worm-like parasites called strongeloids. Eventually the medical officers realised what was causing this problem and they became so knowledgeable on these parasites, that they were able to name the strain of the infection and even the camp where this illness was contracted from.

At Ely RAF hospital we were told one way to eradicate them completely would be to pour boiling water straight down your throat and into your stomach. I'm glad to say and report that I did not suffer such affliction nor did I try such a drastic medical trick but I believe some of those parasites are still wiggling away inside me somewhere today. Needless to say you'll always find me wearing my slippers or shoes nowadays.

ULCERS

Most men suffered ulcers somewhere on their bodies. Many were indeed gross sights with flesh eaten down to the exposed bones, with a putrefied smell that really sickened you; flesh literally dripped from their bodies. It was common to see men having ulcer wounds scraped out with some form of crude implement. The pain would have been immense. Suffice to say a couple or so prisoners would hold a man down whilst he was administered any form of such treatment.

One night an officer said to me, "What's the matter with you?" and I replied telling him I had an ulcer on my toe, which was giving me some real gyp at the time.

A Dutch policeman said "Don't worry, I've got a tablet I can give you to help, but I'll only give you a quarter of it now." So he duly carved up this part of the tablet and told me to dissolve it in some water and carry on like that for four days and that should do the trick in clearing up the ulcer.

This I did, bathing the toe as best I could as the ulcer would for sure travel fast up my leg without some sort of attention... the only bits of bandage we could get hold of had to be washed out, dried straight away in the sun and reapplied, and within time my ulcer fortunately healed itself. If it had not been for the prompt action of those people I would probably have become one of the many amputees in the camp, and there must have been around thirty or more such victims at Chungkai alone by this time. That did not stop the Japs from sending very ill men, men covered from head to toes in jungle sores and boils, scabies and the like, out on the daily working parties. All, no matter their condition of health, had to play their active part in building this wretched railway.

MALARIA

I suffered from this affliction at least seventeen times during my captivity. Insect bites would quickly set this illness off, which would make you feel so cold and shaky but you would sweat profusely. If you could, you would huddle around a fire for warmth in your blanket, or half a blanket in mine and Mort's case. Sadly most of the time all of us who suffered would be forced to work on, the Japanese sparing us no respite whatsoever, having no compassion at all for illness. Remember we were expendable in their eyes.

The Chungkai hospital hut was about 300 yards from the police headquarters away in the far corner where I was often on duty. On several occasions some of us POWs would have to run full pelt down to the hospital to assist the poor boys in the hospital beds who could be heard screaming out at the top of their voices for some help. Crying out, desperately needing respite from their pain caused by cerebral malaria, their brains being badly affected by that strain of virus. Any man seen suffering a fit was a deeply disturbing sight to behold and a haunting sound to listen to, so what must it have been like for those poor suffering men? All of these reminders are still firmly etched in my mind; they will never leave me.

We would rush into their hut, physically hold the poor wretched men down on their beds until a medical officer was found and could arrive to give the man an injection of morphine... if we had any left, that is, and more often than not, with the scant and limited supply that the medical officers were given, this would soon have been used up for one sad case or another. So many men had to endure chronic pain unaided, comforted only by another POW, powerless, despite his deep concern and anguish for his ailing comrade's health.

DYSENTRY

Diarrhoea and dysentery were extremely rife in the camps. Some boys suffered continually, literally day and night and, there was no such luxury as toilet rolls, just foliage, banana leaves or other vegetation if some was left handy nearby and you had the sense to grab it on the run in to the toilet area. My problems were occasional compared to many poor souls who spent countless hours squatting at these latrines, with severe stomach pains. Our degree of sanitation was nothing short of squalid, men covered in their own excrement having little or no control over their bowels. What with our filthy dirty bodies and the stinking pits of latrines to use, this disease was highly contagious and spreading rampantly through the men.

Our "toilets" were about twelve feet long and four feet wide and about ten feet deep into the jungle floor. With bamboo rails across the top for us to hold on to so you didn't slip in, but the weather didn't halt for the sake of using the toilet and during the monsoons it was a treacherous, even perilous, ordeal of a trip. Some men did in fact suffer their peril and death that way, slipping into the latrines to their deaths, being too ill and weak to even grasp onto life. Some bodies were fished out of the trenches but then again several had to be left where they lay. These areas were abominable, absolutely disgusting, fly and maggot ridden stinking pits and no place to dwell, no soap, no towel and no water to even wash your hands in, so you can imagine how quickly these diseases were spreading.

Often we were given the instruction to catch up to 100 flies per day and put them in a jar or old tin, each man having to take his catch and show to the Japs. Such was the speed of epidemics that they spread. They were immensely irritating insects to have to live with, I sadly have the same dislike of flies even today and cannot stay in the room with one, it has to go or die or be well and truly sprayed to death. Hence I have a fly swat to hand for most of the summer months.

There were always hundreds of sick men queuing to use these latrines and as one pit was full up so another one had to be dug and ready for use. Not a task for the faint hearted; an area of indescribable stench that clung to your nostrils and filled the air all around the camps.

The dysentery cases increased and worsened so much so that a hospital had to set up with special wards just for dysentery patients. It is a job to describe the inside of the ward to you. Frankly if you had to pass you would just look inside too scared to venture further to see the poor boys that were lying inside. Fearful of catching a worsening case and having to end up joining them, but basically they had a trench dug straight down through the middle of the huts for their ablutions. These men were far too ill to make it to a nearby latrine. These huts soon became wards of degradation; dried excrement left by one man would some become the platform and bed space of the next unfortunate victim. As I've said many times before sanitation by today's standards had long gone. We were living in absolute squalor.

CHOLERA

This most dreaded of all diseases struck the camp in 1943, we were forbidden to go anywhere near those affected and forbidden to go near water, as the disease was water borne. Men taken into special cholera huts, or shacks as most of these dwellings could be best described, had their haunted eyes sunken into their cheek bones. They must have realised in their heavy hearts that they were effectively done for and feared for their doomed lives. It was bad enough to be segregated and then unceremoniously dumped on the outskirts of the camp itself away from the main huts, but then again many were too ill to realise what was happening to them. It was plain to see when the victim contracted this dreadful illness, convulsions rocked their bodies and they lost complete control of their bodily functions. It was sorrowfully most disturbing to witness.

It hit with such ferocity that up to 19 men from my battalion went into the cholera hut on the one day and all died by nightfall. How much more could we all possibly endure? I wondered how long I would survive, six months maybe... just maybe... A method of testing for cholera was carried out on suspected victims, using a glass tube to collect samples of faeces. Just to see this procedure alone taking place was harrowing enough. With death all around you and many men buried on a daily basis, believe me it is quite a daunting proposition to encounter, truly depressing sights to have witnessed, never in my wildest dreams did I think I would end up living like this.

Some of the POWs had come across a salt water spring up in the mountains and had brought some back for their use. Jim Palfrey and George Sewell being two that I know of. Hence salt in their diet went a long way to preventing them from catching cholera or at least enabling them to recover from it more quickly, should they have fallen victim to this ravaging of all diseases. Salt was actually forced into the victim's mouth by the orderlies as a form of medical cure, but the history books I have read since coming home also concluded that many men were shot by the Japs if hit by this epidemic, to try to stop the spreading of the outbreak even further.

Cholera was rampant in camps for about four weeks or so and certain POWs were assigned to the heart-rending task of creating funeral pyres. Daily collecting the distorted victims from their huts and finally burning their bodies. I saw this happening. I could see plainly the piles of bodies on the pyres, contorting from the heat as the flames took a firm hold and the many corpses lying on the ground in rows waiting to be burnt. We were under strict orders not to go near or to assist, so we had to keep our distance and the Japs certainly kept well away from these areas.

Extra vigilance had to be applied by everyone, by dipping everything into boiling water. Even the Japs were scared stiff of this epidemic which claimed many, many lives, young and old alike. It took no prisoners itself, simply wiping out many good and courageous men in a matter of weeks. It wreaked disastrous havoc amongst our camps and we lost many true friends and comrades to this disease alone!

CHAPTER THIRTEEN

CHUNGKAI 1944

MEN CAGED UP LIKE WILD ANIMALS

Before I left Chungkai camp my Head Officer said to me, "Lockwood, at 2 am. tomorrow morning you have to get some desperately-needed food and water into the 'cooler'."

These so-called "coolers" were bamboo huts about four feet high and four feet wide, so you judge for yourself the sheer discomfort at being landed in one of them. Not enough room for any man to stand up or lay down, men just squatted the best they could. There were six of these coolers crammed into one bigger hut, a prison with-in a prison if you like, and a man would be shoved into this awful cooler as punishment for whatever so-called crime he might have committed. Cooler being the operative word here. They couldn't have been hotter places to be incarcerated in, with temperatures at boiling point for most of the day, let alone the breathless atmosphere in there at night.

Now it was my turn to try to get some much-needed food and water into them to keep them alive as long as we could and hopefully long enough for them to be released from this imprisonment. Their rations of food and water were drastically cut as part of their punishment. The men trapped inside were in a desperate situation.

All this had to be done without being spotted by the Japs of course!

It was a regular thing for a man to spend up to four weeks in a cooler as punishment, not being allowed out at all to stretch his weary limbs. Can you now imagine four weeks scrunched up in such a squatting position? Believe me it's true, it truly took place.

The Japanese handed over the guarding of these coolers to our commanders, and then they still paraded around at about 15 to 20 minute intervals as well.

Japs would walk around these coolers inside the hut at intervals, prodding their wickedly sharp bayonets through the gaps in the bamboo to torment the prisoners even further… men squashed inside stood little or no chance of moving out of the way. The one thing they quickly learned to do was to squeeze over to one side as the Jap was parading around the other, in the vain hope they would escape from being badly cut by the bayonets. But you see beside this torture the prisoners were also being starved, with very little food or water at all and my officer said I was to race across the open space, Jap guard room on the one side and living quarters on the other. I had to collect two dixies, one of food and the other one with water, race back and I mean race back; if I was caught I'd no doubt have to join them in the wretched coolers.

2am on the dot, I did as instructed. This is what I did; collected the dixies from the cookhouse, race back to the hut with the coolers inside, fed them, the six men in turn for one minute each, give them a drink for one minute each, then race back with the empty dixies, all within about a fifteen-minute gap of the Jap guard returning to where I was standing on guard duty outside.

I managed to stand still somehow, being on police duty at just the time the Jap guard passed by me again. I was still out of breath when he came around babbling away "Egumush campo tie" meaning "Everything all right MP?"

Then I immediately asked the question, "You have any babies. Japan sooner, sooner moon. Japan some kind of night sky." Just a load of rubbish and gibberish honestly. I didn't have a clue what to say, just enough really to distract him from my breathlessness.

He sucked it and we had a short but useful conversation of some kind or the other. Neither had a clue what was said but I knew those six men inside the hut felt all the better for what had just happened and that was all that mattered to me.

***

Incidentally, many years after the war ended and when I was in my eighties I attended a Remembrance Service in St. Mary's Church in Bury St Edmunds. I entered the church not knowing many of the FEPOWs present. Age had its effect on looks, I suppose. A man grabbed me and said, "I've just been talking about you, Sid."

I replied that I hoped it wasn't something nasty. He laughed and went on to say, "You saved my life by getting me food and drink whilst I was in the awful cooler back in Chungkai." It was good to see he wasn't starving now.

This man was Percy Buckle, nicknamed Akers, from Rougham. When he was in the cooler, I would suggest he weighed in the region of no more than five stones. Now he is a big fine fellow of a man despite ailing health and in his eighties.

CHAPTER FOURTEEN

SPRING OF 1944

LEFT IN A SHALLOW GRAVE

Another case in Chungkai, which some would say never happened but believe me I was there and can truly bear witness to the following.

Five men escaped from our camp and got as far as Burma. They needed a firearm so they killed a Burmese policeman and took his revolver, only to be given up by the Burmese and recaptured by the Japs.

The five POWs were brought back to camp and chained together and left outside in the open just near the Jap guardroom for a week. I used to see them every day as they lay right outside the Jap guardroom. They were starved and the poor boys nearly went mad in the boiling sun. No food and no water at all for the entire week... then at midnight one night they were taken to the cookhouse and given as much food as they could possibly eat.

I was on duty at the time and alas about 5.30 am early morning I heard some commotion and I saw these poor five men being forced out of camp still in chains, with 72 Jap soldiers and one Japanese officer. I can be sure of those numbers as I stood in the morning twilight and counted them out of camp for myself.

My heart bled for them it seemed like ages but I knew what was coming and within forty-five minutes I later heard that dreaded noise; they had been shot. My friend Mr Bull witnessed it all and ran to the camp to find me to tell me what had happened... when I found him he indicated the Japs arranged the firing squad in a semi circle of the 72 Jap soldiers around the five men.

The five prisoners had been forced to dig their own grave

about 18 inches deep plus they had to make a cross out of bamboo and wire... then the Jap officer gave the command and the five prisoners were shot dead.

I saw the Jap party return and was the first to get out there and see for myself. Mr Bull's account was all too real. My word... what a terrible sight, blood everywhere, boys' legs and arms still not fully in their graves they had dug. I hurried back and got the padre. He was absolutely dumbstruck at what he saw. He then pleaded with the Japs to let us rebury them in the cemetery but not so, we just had to cover them up with some soil and leave them where they lay... what happened to their bodies after I left Chungkai I don't know.

There was arrogance on behalf of the Japs all around us now. Deep ditches had been dug at the perimeter of all our camps, ten feet deep in places and shallowing off to one end, much like silage pits used in farming today, all heavily edged with barbed wire. Bren gun nests were situated also with heavily armed and eager eyed Japanese soldiers at every point, but they didn't seem afraid of outward invasion as the guns were aimed and trained inwards to the camp and at all of us POWs. Obviously if help were to arrive by way of an invasion or whatever means could be mustered by our Allies, then clearly the order would have been given to herd us prisoners into these pits and the rest would have been inevitable history, mass execution; I've no doubt the lot of us would have been shot and already in our mass grave, ready for the covering of soil, much in the same way as the five comrades had been mown down earlier and left in their shallow graves.

We were told by our own officers that the first men in the trenches stood the better chances of survival, effectively being shielded by those shot down above us. As long as you could get a clear airway you could possibly endure and survive the onslaught that was truly thought might happen. But we could have no drill for this eventuality, no practice run or preparation, just to hang on to the belief and hope that it would not come to such a disastrous end, but then again men were already being executed regularly, taken away from under our noses, so we would be spared nothing, that's for sure, if any rescue attempts had been made.

CHAPTER FIFTEEN

1943 - 1944

PANTOMIMES AND FOOTBALL

If any of this disaster in our so-called story of history could be called "light-hearted", then the pantomimes and concerts certainly brought a little light into an otherwise very gloomy situation

Leo Britt and Anthony Quinn soon became quite expert at putting on wonderful concert parties. These took place about once a month. Two of the stage performances were called "Wonder bar" and another was called "Night must fall". The men involved in this entertainment were our heroes as they worked alongside us on the lines during the day, returned for their evening rations of rice, attended the obligatory parade and then promptly set about making plans for the shows. Rehearsing and practising well into the small hours of the morning, and all for our entertainment and pleasure for the coming shows.

They even managed to make the set look authentic, creating a proper stage and all the props they could muster. We owed all of them a great debt for their efforts which was appreciated by many, even our captors.

Men were chosen from amongst the prisoners if they had any musical flair about them, some playing accordions, mouth organs and guitars. It never ceased to amaze us what they could come up with or where they had stowed their gear and equipment.

Costumes were all cleverly hand made out of vegetation, or anything they could pinch from the local natives They would have pinched the shoe laces out of your shoes but alas many of us had long worn shoes out. Their efforts were splendid given all the circumstances.

These concerts would be watched by about a 1000-strong crowd of prisoners all sitting on the ground and usually took place around 8pm and lasted about two hours. Men would join in the singing, albeit in a subdued way, many thinking of home, many thinking of survival, but they all entered into the spirit of the show to the best of their ability, and the efforts of the organisers lifted our souls to endure another day of captivity in the jungle.

The Japs would sit around and watch these concerts with us, until one day they suspected the performers had a wireless set on stage. This was merely a prop but it caused big, big problems. We were in deep trouble; it looked enough like a wireless for them to react as usual.

Concerts were eventually banned altogether, due probably to the suspect wireless, and so indeed were church services; these had long been banned.

The weather was so diverse that at one time and for months on end it would rain and rain, and the rivers would be in full flood, followed by such intense heat that the river would quickly dry out in places. I recall only to vividly one day 30 feet deep down, in a dry part of the river bed on the River Kwai how 2000 men, many very ill, wounded, lame and totally exhausted, coming down for a church service which had been incredibly arranged for us under the guise of a “pantomime”; do remember both had been totally banned by now.

As the first hymn struck up, with our defiant voices lifting into the jungle surrounds, the Jap guards came racing down like absolute madmen, charging with fixed bayonets pushing down the aisle or gap through between the men and straight towards the padre at the front leading the service. My heart sank and Don Dawson and I both prayed aloud, "Please don’t let them kill this man, our padre."

Just one foot from him... they stopped, their only intention was to kill him for leading our service, but he spoke out in a commanding voice and said, "Father forgive them for they know not what they do."

It was a very chilling and extremely frightening moment but the padre was mercifully spared his life and we thanked God for that. This service was a far cry from how we started our church services in the earlier days at Chungkai. There we built an open arena type of church area and it was attended if only by some handful of men along with our padre. Don Dawson, Victor Mortlock and others including myself would go along for our service, having the mickey taken out of us by our comrades shouting, "Bring us a bit of cake back" but we were not dissuaded from our witness.

Church services were strictly abandoned altogether, actually forbidden to take place by the Japs, but on this occasion my heart was lifted to see our congregation had grown from a handful of witnesses to a strong crowd of around 2000 men. Prisoners showing defiance at breaking the Japanese rules, but hopefully men also in need of God's grace in such desperate times and conditions.

Hearts turned by the sad ravages and acts of war, I hope and pray many of those men who witnessed those terrifying scenes in the river bed of the Kwai still maintain their faith in God above today, if they are lucky enough like me to still be around.

We were then dismissed to our huts for disobeying a fire alarm of all things; something we had never heard of over the previous two years, but that was the Japs' excuse for breaking up our church service.

FOOTBALL AND CRICKET

Football along with cricket took place near Chungkai but only after the building of the railway was completed. We wouldn't have won a trophy or the Ashes mind you, but we all joined in as and when we could.

Many sick men who could summon the energy used to kick a football about (now just where did that ball come from, where had the ball been hidden all that while or again was it stolen from the local natives?). We had no shoes but the camaraderie certainly lifted the morale and even the Japs were OK about this sport being played on a clearing used for our parade ground, just outside the huts.

CHAPTER SIXTEEN

JUNE 1944

SCENERY, WILDLIFE AND THE WEATHER

The monsoons were I think the worst of the elements to contend with, lasting some seven months overall, I reckon. You got to know when the monsoons were arriving as the wind really started to blow, whipping through any remaining tree tops, howling as it blew. We prisoners would hang on to our huts for dear life; otherwise we would have lost them completely to the winds alone. It was commonplace then to have twenty-four hours of rain, for four weeks on end, torrential downpours of rain, before the sun would break through for a while and then off it would go again, rain, rain and yet more rain. As the waters came down the floods came up and so it went on.

We would wake up in the mornings with our hut floors awash, roofs leaking and waters rising and to see and hear the river in full flood rushing on by. Huge trees uprooted and floating past like matchsticks. Such was the force and rush of the water even houses, local kampongs as they were known, could be seen churning down the river with their owners still clinging perilously on to what they owned. People swiftly floating past, trying to clamber on to wreckage or boats in their way, desperately trying to stay alive and survive the elements alone.

When the river was calm, it had a peaceful and eerily quiet beauty surrounding it, but it was a common sight to see the local people going up and down river with their dhows, selling their wares. So this river was a local route for traders and much used by those living by the banks. Indeed the river was used to its fullest potential by the Japs moving their fuel, arms, ammunition and stores up and down the river, visiting camp by camp using barges and boats of all shapes and sizes. So it was a common sight to see a party of men going down to the river bed, complete with bamboo poles slung over their shoulders to help offload whatever stores had arrived, clamber their way back up the river embankment and make back for camp, complete with their guards muttering and chuntering away behind them.

Morning mists rising off the jungle canopy were also a sight to behold; this was really a beautiful country to be in, but not under these dreadful circumstances of war.

That railway had to be built at all costs, according to our Japanese captors. The monsoons made our labour and working conditions even harder, with only a loin cloth to wear and nothing else. Mud squelching everywhere, all churning up a quagmire so that you could not avoid being filthy dirty and of course exhausted, only to return at night to a sodden hut and your usual bed space area with just half a wet blanket for the night's cover.

No pillow to rest your head and no mattress to ease the aching bones, no lighting of any kind, just a very hard bamboo surface to lay upon but I managed to endure and survive like this for three and a half years, and so mercifully, thank God, did many others.

The dawn usually came around 6 am and dusk fell around 8 pm or thereabouts. Some of the lads had rigged up a few coconut oil lamps with some form of wick but these were very limited and not in all huts. When it was dark it was really dark, except for the moonlit nights, which were very bright indeed. If you were to have been lucky enough to have had a newspaper with you, which we didn't of course, you would certainly have been able to read it quite plainly by the moonlight, or the parish lantern as we call it back home, but mainly the moon shone upon the haggard and drawn faces of men trying to sleep through total exhaustion.

Mostly the nights felt long and dark, occasionally men quietly exchanging the news of the day, what had happened to whom and how friends were coping, but mainly it was just the sounds of the jungle and its weird noises, and of men shuffling back and forth. Either we were unable to sleep or for the obligatory trip to the latrines, if we could make it of course; although the floor of our huts was bare earth you could still hear feet plodding back and forth at all hours. It was during these darkest of hours that your mind would take you back home, wondering how the folks were, how were they coping with the war, were they still all right. Then the darkest of thoughts would follow. Were they still alive, did they know of my dilemma? Your imagination would run riot and it's true to say it didn't help one little bit to ponder on such thoughts. It was just terrible not knowing a thing. You just had to cling to hope and pray to God that all was well with your loved ones.

The Japs used to wear some type of trench coats for protection during these monsoons but frankly you didn't feel like looking at them let alone take in what their apparel was. Suffice to say it was far superior to ours at the time.

One story I can add in here and share with you, is that one night I was coming down with some other POWs between the line of Japs back to our huts and, yes, some of these Japs were a little more friendly to us than others, and I could see that this Jap soldier was asleep. I saw plainly that he had nodded off whilst on duty. We were unknowingly being followed quite closely at the time by another Jap officer who spotted the trouble immediately, so it's a good job we didn't go over to him and wake him or speak to him in any way, otherwise what was about to follow would have surely landed us in serious trouble. The Jap behind us went over to the sleeping Jap and went absolutely mad. He picked up the man's rifle and hit him fiercely right on top of his head so hard and violently, such was the brutality of his action that the man died four days later, presumably caused by a fractured skull.

Now back to the weather, the other five months of the year weather-wise, we would have to contend with intense heat, intolerable temperatures 100 degrees in the shade, so to speak. If you had a hat you surely made sure you took it with you everywhere you went.

We were tanned to say the least, black in fact and often mistaken for Indians. Scores of times I was stopped and poked by Japs asking me if I was an Indian in their language. It must have been my raven-black hair. It certainly wasn't my muscles as I didn't have many left.

The River Kwai never dried up completely during these dry periods of intense heat, but parts of the river bed certainly were exposed, especially around the overflow areas were the flooding had chewed away at the softer sides of the river banks, leaving big swathes of dry dusty areas. So what could be a swell of twenty or thirty feet of waters rushing its way past, could soon in a matter of days with the force of the sun and heat, become a dusty dry river bed area.

There was to be no respite during the day from the intensity of the sun, no sun oil that we wallow in today for our bare backs. All the trees, from what was originally an impenetrable forest, had been felled by our hands to make way for the rail bed, so our only shade was that of our huts back at camp at night. All too often it was dusk before we made it back; by then it was already somewhat cooler than the working day.

The landscape was indeed very beautiful. Water melon fields were abundant and also there was a lot of rice being grown in the paddy fields. I was privileged, remember, being in the police at Chungkai, as I managed to walk over and around those areas scores of times. I was there one afternoon and was stopped by a local Chinese man who wanted to know if I wanted to listen to his radio. Not so, my friend, no thank you. If he happened to be a Jap my head would be rolling in those paddy fields.

Bananas were growing all around the areas we were in. If we came close enough to any to cut them down, they would be taken back for ripening but mostly these plantations belonged to the Thai people, so pickings were a bit of a rarity.

The jungle ahead was thick intense vegetation and by now we had swathed and carved our way through, cutting down beautiful species of trees of every kind, rubber trees, coconut, bamboo, hardwood trees of teak and mahogany, some seventy feet tall, all demolished for the Japs' railway. Once trees were felled they would be floated down river to the sawmills and sawn into sleepers for the party of gangs to lay the line behind us, the so-called clearing party, that I was working with.

Across the valleys were breathtaking views and sights but a lot of the terrain was to be consumed to the Japanese greed and pace of building this railway, that nothing but nothing stood in their way. If it had to be uprooted or destroyed so be it; they had a captured prisoner workforce of men to do it with.

The locals had precious little anyway by way of personal possessions. Their homes were nothing more than bamboo shacks dotted around where we were working. There were no brick buildings of any kind whatsoever around for miles and miles. These people really did live in the back of beyond, maybe with the odd chicken or two for company.

As far as the wildlife was concerned you could hear the dingoes howling at night along with the tiger cats. These animals were quite tame I guess, desperate for food more likely, but little did these creatures know they'd come to the wrong place. We were more likely to eat them than the other way around. I was quite close to one on one occasion when a mate of mine, Bill Procter who was in the police with me, killed one with a catapult.

Incidentally Bill, as I've mentioned before, managed to get out and about more than most. Being much more daring he used to say to me, "Sid, you know where I am if they want me, don't you." Maybe he bought the catapult from a native, who knows, but he put it to effective use against this animal. Often he used to slip out of camp and visit a kampong about a mile away. He was very friendly with those people. What used to happen was, this family used to put him on a boat attached to a rope, whereupon he would lie down on the bottom of the boat. They would push him out into the River Kwai complete with the daily English newspapers for him to read and digest. Once he had read all the news, he would tug on the rope to alert them he was ready and they would haul him back to shore. On his return to camp he could let the officers know of any bombings or advance by the enemy, but what a risk he took. If a man needed a battery for a hidden and forbidden wireless, he was your man, he could get his hands miraculously on anything; hence the catapult.

Every night he would say to me "Come on, Sid, you know where we are going." Sure enough we would go towards the rivers edge to collect pebbles. This particular evening, with a dog howling across the way for all its might, he said, "I'm gonna have that ol` dog boy."

I said, "Are you, do you reckon so?" Yes, sure enough, he

got out his catapult and with one aim, one stone, there lay one dead dog, right outside the Jap guard room. Next morning the Japs went mad, us not daring to go anywhere near the dead animal of course and certainly Bill was not laying claim to his shooting ability.

Nevertheless the Japs were cute enough to notice the stone right by the dead dog, so out they rushed, screaming and yelling at us, searching every hut and man for a catapult. They weren't quick enough for Bill though. He had legged it to the cookhouse and swiftly burnt his catapult on the cookhouse fires, knowing very well he could soon renew that source of weapon supply. This poor man became very ill indeed towards the end of the war and my friend Jim Palfrey was witness to a harrowing operation on his skull. The illness would have killed him before the war ended, according to the medical officers at the time. So they all agreed they had no option but to operate and very crudely at that, I guess. Sharpened up teaspoons were the only implements available and three willing men to hold poor Bill on the operating table, before mercifully, thank God, they successfully removed the offending growth. I'm more than pleased this dear man made it home to his loved ones but apparently died in the 1990s.

Back to the wildlife and the animals who shared their jungle with us. We didn't get to see that many monkeys in the jungle but you could hear them chattering and screaming away in the jungle tree tops in the distance. Perhaps they were cursing us for taking their habitation away. You would maybe just glimpse them whilst working on the line, them scuttling from tree to tree, but little by way of close encounters.

Crocodiles also joined us with the swimming and bathing in the River Kwai. Seriously, we kept a very wary eye out for these predators, although think of the shoes we could have made had we been courageous and strong enough to catch one of those big fellows!

There were plenty of snakes around. A native caught one bluish-grey whopper and dragged it to the edge of camp and it was laid outside the Jap guard room for us to go and see. It was over thirty feet long and as round as a big dinner plate, with a head on it like the size of a bullock, massive thing. Perhaps they ate it, who will ever know?

Once there was a cobra underneath a pile of bamboo and this snake was causing, as you can imagine, quite a stir amongst us all. Naturally the Japs ordered the POWs to go and shift the pile of bamboo. They wouldn't have cared if the cobra struck out at one of us as long as it avoided them. The Japs were so scared of this snake, do you know, unbelievably, they gave one of my mates a rifle and told him to shoot it. Luckily he didn't take aim at them, he tried to attempt to do as he was commanded... but we all said to shoot it would be the wrong way, but rather to hit it hard with a stick and sideways on and obviously quickly before it could strike out with its venom. The cobra hustled out from the bamboo and sat up, its menacing head swaying from side to side right ready to strike. I was only about two feet away when the boys were quickly in with the sticks and killed it stone dead, thank the Lord. That little rascal had caused a commotion, I can tell you.

One night a blue snake shot out from under my bed area. Something roused me, I woke up and out he went, scuttling along the edge of the hut. That one was about three foot long. You would often be disturbed by some creature or insect landing right on top of you, dropping from the roof of the huts, spiders and ants in abundance, so you see the nights were quite eventful too.

Black scorpions were another common creature to encounter. There were scores of them running and crawling around. The boys would soon be after them, killing them as soon as looking at them for fear of being bitten by the things. Still one thing for sure, we didn't have to check inside our boots for scorpions because we didn't have any boots!

Rats, strangely enough, were not to be widely seen, not even at the infamous toilet areas. I'd hate to think this is because we had consumed most of them. I'll put it down to so many men being about, that they would kill anything. Perish the thought that I may have eaten one!

Flying foxes were often seen, birds too, beautifully coloured parrots, but these were quickly moving on because of the noise around from the gangs of men hard at work.

Believe it or not, even vultures lurked around whilst the men were working away, ugly-looking birds circling around us, perhaps hoping they could get to a corpse and rend it apart before we could bury the victim or take the body back to camp for burial. Even great big fruit bats zoomed over our heads and used to hang about in the evenings.

Frogs could be heard croaking away all the times. These were much bigger than our species back home in England.

Beautifully coloured butterflies could often be seen, much larger than most of our species back in England.

So all in all the landscape and its surrounding areas of untouched jungle were of a strange beauty, but we couldn't dwell on such thoughts for many minutes. Our life was all about survival, and it was honestly only to be the fittest and luckiest of us that would live to see the green fields of England again. I kept on praying I would be amongst the lucky ones and make it safely home.

CHAPTER SEVENTEEN
1944 - 1945

ALLIED BOMBINGS AND WORKING WITH ELEPHANTS

Chungkai camp was asked to send yet more fit men up the line. I use the word "fit" quite literally you realise. Hence from amongst the working parties there were insufficient so-called fit men to make up the required numbers, so the officers had to draw from the military police and I was then on the move again. Up the line to Konkuita this time, if I thought I had been hard done by so far then little did I realise the evil that I was about to face.

On occasions Allied bombers dropped leaflets explaining how the war was progressing but we were forbidden to pick them up, being told if we did, we would be shot. Having witnessed so much for so long I have no reason to doubt that threat at this time in my captivity.

Moving up from Chungkai to Konkuita was a further one hundred miles or more. We were sent by boat, some 90 of us POWs travelling for over a day on the river. It was at this point that the railroad from the north built mainly by Australians and Indians met up with our track from the south to form the complete railway line from Thailand to Burma. Some 256 miles approximately in total and laid with 90000 wooden sleepers. Sleepers in number, as the history of this railway unfolded, that would represent one for every life lost in captivity. After this line was completed heavy bombing raids started up. It was soon apparent the Japs were getting pretty petrified by this time too, which only served to make them more determined and stronger in their defiance. All the time we were becoming weaker and weaker through the treatment handed down to us.

It was now our own people destroying the railway we had build by hand and the bridges came under severe attack and raids happened regularly for about six months late on in 1944 to mid 1945. Our work soon became a prime target for the overhead bombers and their raids soon became deadly accurate. As the bombers came over the Japs soldiers were the first to leg it and scarper into the jungle surroundings, shouting at us as they hurtled past that they would slit all our throats before the Americans arrived. We had no reason to disbelieve them from what murderous activities we had witnessed so far to date. The threats were as real as they were years ago!

Bombers continually hitting the rail lines, ammunition trucks, stores and more, several of our own men, many of whom were not quick enough to make it into the jungle from the rail clearings were killed, hence again many needless deaths occurring but this time through the actions of our allies.

We were quickly set to task, back in gangs to repair the damage and back to rebuilding the railway. Still nothing mechanical to hand despite the obvious urgency on behalf of our captors, but the annoying part was lines of prisoners working on the railway line were being gunned down by Allied bombers. Little did those in the air know what was happening on the ground and this work was spread over some 20 to 30 miles, repairing lines day after day for several months and as soon as repairs were made and the line working again, it would be bombed again and again. At this point in time I actually helped to repair the bridges, which up until now I had not been involved with, but what needless pain this war was causing.

Even though we couldn't escape, believe me, in our way we did every thing we could possibly get away with, in hampering the progress of their blessed railway being sped up by their constant barracking and bellowing of "speedo," speedo."

Part of our duties was to unload the many boats that used to pull alongside the jetty into our area where our camp was nearby.

One occasion when we were emptying one of many boats that had arrived at the river side, we cunningly planned a massive explosion. It went like this... a tug of sorts would be heard churning its way up the river towards our camp, complete with three barges in tow. This morning at 7am we had our orders to go down to unload fuel. FUEL, unbelievable, this fitted in nicely with our little plot. This was to be our golden chance to cause as much havoc as we could and so a plan was hastily hatched up.

The way the barges were to be emptied, or so we were told was, some POWs were set to work on board the barges, which were full of 45-gallon barrels of fuel, petrol and diesel. They had to manhandle the barrels to the edges of the barges, load them or attach them onto our pulley rope system, which the Japs had helped us to rig up, all for us to haul the barrels thirty feet up the river bank. So we worked in pairs, two men side by side on the ropes pulling for all their worth and might, so thirty men were set to work on the river bank, whilst some others were on board the barges.

Those on board of course were in on our plan and at the command; they would dive into the river and get clear of the boat. As the plan was to send a barrel back down the embankment, quicker than we could pull it upwards, thus causing the explosion on board the barges.

I was the Joe Muggins that set the ball in motion, me. It was agreed I was to slip first, my partner second, and then the whole line of men on the river bank involved in the hauling process would cascade down the slope and fall over and away from the planned explosion. At the same time those on board the barge were to dive into the river to safety. This plan was all hastily fed through to all involved in readiness for us to stand back and watch the firework show.

Our time had arrived. It was 7am one morning when we all knew we could now win this part of the war on our own, or so we thought, at the given sign 2.15pm as pre-arranged, and having asked the guarding Japs beside us for the time, I did as planned. Whilst we were counting, itche, nee, san, see, we were effectively counting, one, two, three, four, (whereas back home we go one, two, three, the Japs had to be different and add number four) being about the seventh pair back, I missed my footing right on cue, slipped downwards and let go of the ropes, shouting as I fell to warn the rest, my mate went flying, so did the rest of the hauling party, and whoosh!... down went the barrel, bouncing and crashing its way to the river, men on board the barges dived into the River Kwai and our barrel lumped against the barges full of petrol and up she went... NO... not so... Chaos ensued for a minute or so, but it ended more like a damp squib really, nothing happened, tough old barrels or bad planning boys! We had failed, the barrel did not explode and our plot was laid wide open for the Japs to deal with as only they know how!!

To our utter amazement, up jumped the Jap who had been lying bemused beside us all the while, I could have touched him at times as we hauled on the ropes. He came over to us all and very calmly said "Listen hear you guys [in very posh English], I was educated in Cambridge and I've heard every word you have all said this morning, I can speak perfect English and I therefore understand every thing about your little so-called plot. I know what you have been trying to do, but I'll tell you this, don't come it when I'm on guard over you. Just behave yourselves; I know who is going to win the war now. All you've got to do is to look after yourselves and keep out of trouble. I'll let you all off this time but never ever try a stunt like that again whilst I'm around." We felt as small as church mice! ... The barrel didn't even split, we hadn't caused any damage at all, so we carried on working again realising that not only do walls have ears, but so does the jungle too!!... He's heard everything. So that was to be our pathetic attempt at sabotage, but if we had pulled it off, it would have been a terrific explosion wouldn't it... I just thanked my lucky stars it was him and not Osour or Moonface on guard at the time. They would have had my head right clean off, that they would, no messing about either, no arguing the toss, it would have been curtains for me and the others too I guess ...

Yet further atrocious happenings were about to unfold in this hell hole of Konkuita.

The truth of my story is this, every morning when we left the camp to go along to the docks. Not docks as we would expect to see today, but an area where the boats would tie up to a jetty type pier to unload whatever their cargo was at the time. All equipment still needed for the war effort for the Japs to use, or rather for us to use on their behalf.

We formed up in the chain gang near to a boat down by the

jetty, as we were to unload boxes of ammunition this particular day. When we left the camp with the sergeant in charge in the morning, he was always supposed to detail two men to fall out and stay behind to clean up the Jap living quarters. This was a renowned happening but on this day we had a sergeant with us named Nobby Clarke, who was out of the Royal Corp of Signals. He was a kind man to us. He had left camp with us all early in the day, but came away and he never told two men to stay behind for the cleaning up process.

However, the dreaded Osour appeared at 10 o'clock right bang on tea break time. He went straight over to Sergeant Clarke and made it quite clear that his instructions had not been obeyed and his house had not been cleaned. Osour kept asking Nobby why he hadn't followed instructions, until in the end Nobby admitted he had not asked anyone to do the task that morning.

What with that the Jap guards, Moonface and Osour, set about giving Nobby a good hiding. The viciousness of their attack make you feel utterly sick in the stomach, they were kicking and hitting him so severely. We were made to sit on the ground, George Marritt close by me. These Japs were giving this poor man such a heavy bashing, we kept yelling at Nobby not to go down on the floor as this always made the matter much worse for the victim, but to try and take the punishment and bear it out, see it through to the end, so to speak. Sadly he eventually fell down to the ground, the worst thing he could have done at the time, sadly he couldn't take any more.

Whereupon the Japs turned him on his back and proceeded to jump up and down on his stomach. Both Japs at the same time would land right on top of the man. We could only see them killing him, so much was their fury and rage that I really thought Nobby's intestines would be squashed and come out of his rear end.

These Japs were raving mad but so was I. I jumped up in a boiling fit. I didn't say anything to George and he didn't say anything to me. We both jumped up off the ground together. Enough was enough. We had already seen too much of this kind of thing going on, and I just couldn't take any more, or witness any more, without speaking out. Or should I say shouting out.

I went over and shouted at these Japs saying, "Pack it in. This is no way to treat a British soldier, even if we are prisoners of war.

Pack it in; we don't treat people like this back in our country." What with that, to my utter surprise they immediately stopped.

They ordered someone to carry out the obligatory antidote and to fetch a pail of water to throw over Nobby. This was done and then the usual thing happened, about fifty or so men, those most near to the Jap guards, were ordered to form up in three ranks. We were to be counted yet again, don't ask me why, it was a regular occurrence, but we fifty would be only those nearest to the guards out of a great mass of men working away at the dock area.

They briskly and abruptly lined us up and counted us off. I was standing in the middle rank.

Osour had told me back at Chungkai that he wanted to become a Gunso, which is a higher ranking officer than he already was. He was the equivalent to a third class private, but he so much wanted promotion so therefore when he got the chance, he was going to show his ability and his time had arrived; it was now his turn to bask in glory.

Osour, Moonface and two or three more Japs paraded up and down our lines, inspecting us POWs. Osour inspected the front rank, then commanded the front rank to take two paces forward so that he had more room to inspect the second row, mine! Osour got to me. He looked and he looked, he stared at me for some moments, chilling it was, as his eyes went up and down me several times, always returning to my face, but I could hear my heart pounding in my own ears. Then he went on past a few feet and stopped. I immediately thought that's it, he's after me, I just had that awful sinking feeling in the pit of my stomach again, my heart then missed several beats, I can tell you. He came back to me, looked me straight in the eyes and said, "You were at Chungkai, weren't you?" I obviously said I was. Then he went on to question how long I had been at Konkuita and I confirmed three months.

Then Osour went on to say, "You are a Christian, aren't you?" to which I replied "Yes". Good gracious, my fear was swiftly confirmed; they immediately set about me in the middle of the rank, both of these guards, Moonface and Osour. One other Jap stood behind me and as I went backwards so he would push me forwards to take another bashing. They knocked me about back and forth for about eight minutes. Osour left off hitting me, then asked me, "Now are you still a Christian?"

So I replied, "Yes, I am still a Christian." Whereupon they started the treatment up again and further bashing and pushing around took place, only their aim was more deadly and accurate each time.

They beat me and knocked me almost senseless, my limbs were bruised to the bone and I was trying not to go down, having witnessed Sergeant Clarke take his punishment. I knew only too well what these men were capable of, and in my mind I didn't want them bouncing on top of my stomach two at a time. They stopped again and asked me the same question for a third time, "Are you still a Christian?"

This time I shouted the reply back, "YES I've always been a Christian and I always shall be!"

My yelled reply echoed around the men watching but the beatings carried on. A little man called Bill Spalding made the men sit down and watch and shouted at me to say I was not a Christian so the beatings would cease. He went on to say, "We all know you are a Christian, Sid, so for goodness' sake save your own life. They'll kill you otherwise."

I managed to reply, "They won't kill me."

But back came his honest and truthful reply, "They'll kill you, Sid." He was saying something I didn't want to hear or believe, but how much more could I endure. It was now becoming a total blur.

Eventually after some twenty or more minutes of this continually bashing, hitting me viciously around the head, straight in the face and eyes, even punching me in the stomach, kicking me hard in the back, legs, you name it, and even in the unmentionables with their sturdy boots on, time and time again, I was miraculously still on my feet, don't ask me how. I was going round in circles, now totally dazed and almost out for the count, battered, bleeding and very bruised and for a fourth and final time Osour asked me the same question to which I replied, "OK, I'm not a Christian then," and the beatings stopped immediately. They had won yet again!

I went down and lay where I was, only to my horror to see them grab George and frog march him away. My heart sank thinking they were going to shoot him. I could hear George shouting back at us that he would never give in, never give in and so his voice went into the distance. The further he was marched away him, still murmuring back to us that he would never give in. I listened for the shot but it didn't follow so I feared they would bayonet him to death. I'd had it. I thought my time would end there and then and George's too.

The boys came to my aid in the usual way, pail of cold water job and some tender loving care and there I lay until about midday. The charwallah brewing the tea nearby kept a close eye on me whilst the other men had to return to work in the chain gang. Later on I was also instructed to return to the gang to work on, so off I crawled.

I was just about able to walk by then so went hobbling back to unloading the stores from the boats. Our blokes were so cute and there is no mistaking it, that they had some empty boxes at the ready for such people as me, recent victims in other words. I was not the only one to receive such treatment. Many of us took severe beatings, so when it was my turn to lift a heavy box of ammunition; they lifted an empty box on my shoulders so I could zigzag up the thirty foot bank from the river with relative ease. Japs standing close by were totally unaware of this planned protection from further pain. The men offloading from our shoulders would pretend the boxes looked heavy to keep up the charade. That's how I carried on until 5 o'clock in the evening.

At 5 o'clock I thought right, I'm going to get in the front queue this time, so when we were told to left turn I would be on the right hand side of the road as we marched back to camp. Knowing that on my right hand side was a malaria ditch all the way back to the camp, I was hopeful that I would find my mate George. I looked intently but couldn't spot him, not a thing all the way back to camp, but as I walked and stumbled my way back to camp I realised how lucky I was still to be alive, looking at the columns of men with me all trudging back to camp, many men being carried on stretchers by mates, them being too ill and too weary to even walk.

On return to camp we had the usual search to see if we had pinched anything. Once the Jap Officer gave the "dismiss" we all scattered off to our huts. To my big surprise and sheer delight, as

I walked back to mine, there sat George cross-legged on the bed just inside the doorway.

What a total relief to see him still alive! After checking he was all right, he went on to explain they marched him back to camp and told him to stay in the hut and not go out even to the toilet. He went on to ask me how I was of course; saying that I had really taken a hard bashing but both agreed it was all over now. We were still alive so we agreed to go down to the river together to have our evening wash.

After our bathe, we went back to our huts as it was time for tea, then evening parade. On parade that evening the Jap officer in charge had an interpreter with him. He went up to the rostrum and all the other Jap officers had to bow to him as usual. The counting was completed by our own officers, that is those officers that had not been rounded up and locked up themselves. Many of our officers took very severe punishment indeed, but for those who did take command they carried out their counting duties as still the Japs couldn't count, and hut numbers were to be agreed one by one.

The interpreter then took the rostrum and wailed out, "Listen to me you English b's I want the two men who caused all the trouble down at the docks today to come forward." I took root on the spot so did George, motionless, riveted and afraid once again.

Bear in mind not all the men on parade had even the slightest idea of what he was referring to, not having all been in our gang at the docks anyway, but of course several men were aware of our identity. The interpreter called for us to go forward a second time. Still we remained silent. He then said, "We know who you are and if you don't come forward, we'll come into the ranks and fetch you out."

Our immediate mates said, "Go on, Sid and George, go and get it over with, you'll only make matters worse for yourselves," them thinking we were in for yet another bashing.

So reluctantly we both stepped forward, feeling awful and totally wretched, walking out in front of the whole parade. We made out way to the front, bowed as expected, whereupon he asked us if we knew why we had been called out. "No, we don't know," came our reply but he soon relayed to all that we had caused enormous trouble down at the docks this morning.

This fearless man then went on to relay to the hushed troops standing on duty, that it had been decided that we were both to be court-martialled, executed!.. I froze... but somehow both George and I found our voices and went on and questioned his decision and asked why. He replied, "What you did was incitement to mutiny." We strongly disagreed with him, but there was no room to reason with this man, he only firmly reiterated his decision. Stating that we had stopped the Jap guards from doing their duty, in other words giving Nobby a bashing and trouncing like that was their "duty".

The interpreter went on to state we would be court-martialled, executed, presumably shot, in four days' time. In the meanwhile we were to lie at the feet of the Japs in their guard room. No sooner he finished his declaration than we were manhandled and physically dragged away and bundled roughly off to the Jap guard room. They slung us in the room quite literally and dumped us down on their floor like two bags of potatoes, to await our fate... now I truly was afraid for my life. This was to be the end of my war!

Everything rushes and floods back into your mind then I can tell you, Mum and Dad, Joyce, my brothers and sisters, family, loved ones, friends, now will we ever see them again, not if the Japs had their way now with this planned execution!

This Jap guard room housed twenty-four guards, all moving around, with space for eighteen beds, and consisted of three rows of six men, sleeping and resting at one time, with the other six out on duty. Back row, middle row and front row all fearsome and heavily armed Jap guards. Every two hours these 24 men changed guard, six were out on duty, six moving forward a row every two hours and so forth until it was the front row's turn to take the guard outside. They didn't exactly work long shifts, did they? Here we were to lie for the next four mentally torturing days, watching all this activity and movement of our captors, and not allowed to even talk to each other, incarcerated in a room full of hostility and fear.

We weren't there long before a couple of our mates brought over our blankets from our huts, along with our dixies, well at least a blanket and my remaining half blanket left to me by

Victor. Grasping these two precious commodities it wasn't long before the British officer came over to us. Obviously we stood up to attention when he arrived.

He asked us both to give an account of ourselves. We explained. He went on to say that he had been pleading with the Japanese officers to have us both released, only to confirm they would not hear of it and the court martial would go ahead as planned. He said he was sorry he had not succeeded and that he would continue trying and then bade us goodnight, wishing us the best of British luck as he left us there.

As ordered by the Jap soldiers, down we laid on the hard floor again. Next morning there was a Captain Riley come in to see us both. He had been ordered to sit behind us but he was not to speak with either of us. So there he silently sat, hour after hour to witness everything that went on. We had nothing to eat or drink the first night, but were given a small amount of rice the next day. Still we laid there, the British officer returned once more enquiring how we had got on and still stated he was doing his best to get us off this charge, but our case seemed doomed.

On day two, one of the Jap guards got up and put his boot sharply into me, whereupon I jumped up to my feet. Amazingly he gave me three dollars and said I was to go to a Thai kampong for a bottle of whisky but I wasn't to go out through the main gate but go outside via the jungle cutting and this kampong would be about a mile away from camp.

Off I went all alone, realising as I walked that if I met up with some other guards they would have shot me for being out of camp anyway. So it was a wary and bizarre journey to say the least. I kept my wits about me, though. I just hoped I didn't encounter a tiger or snake along the track. The Jap had told me to walk into the native's hut, tell him I wanted whisky and all would be OK. It was and I got a small tot of saki to drink there and then. I didn't speak to him any more nor he me. I returned to camp and got back through the fence to return to the Jap guard room complete with his bottle of whisky.

As I was walking sheepishly back through the camp I met a man called Cooper. He was in the carriers with me, but he clearly didn't want to stop to speak with me, he briefly even told me so. Knowing full well the consequences of a court martial killing and being caught talking to such a man was out of the question. I told him to shut up and listen to me and that I wanted him to do something for me.

I hurriedly went on to say, "When you get home I want you to go to Cockfield between Bury St Edmunds and Sudbury for me and ask for the Lockwood family in the village. There was only the one family by that name. Tell my father we did what we thought to be right... just those eight words." Cooper would be going home; I knew I wouldn't be as day four and the dreaded court martial was looming. I was desperate to get a message home somehow, so I proceeded on with the bottle of whisky for the Jap and continued to lie on the floor of the guardroom, deep in thought hoping he had grasped the urgency of my message for folks back home.

On day three the British officer came back to us, challenging us if we knew exactly what would be happening with the court martial, him reiterating the Japs would go into a frenzy, not understanding our language, making us stand, then kneel and eventually slashing off our heads with one of their mighty swords. Having made himself perfectly clear, thank you, sir, he continued to say he was yet still trying to get us off. I certainly prayed long and hard, I can tell you.

At 6 o'clock that evening George whispered to me that he could hear someone taking a real beating, I could hear it too. This went on for about an hour. All went quiet for a short while and as I looked out of the Jap guard room door I could see this figure staggering towards us, like some cowboy in the western films. It was our British officer.

The Japanese emperor had ordered that fifty "fit" men leave Konkuita at 10 o'clock that evening but the officer was trying to explain he could not make up the numbers and must therefore take the two prisoners out of the Jap guardroom to complete his numbers. For this he received his severe beating and stood up to his punishment until they relented and said to take George and myself out to make up the numbers that night. Good thinking on behalf of our officer and true bravery as well, knowing he would be punished for even suggesting such a thing, but on this miraculous occasion he won the day for us.

The major said that one more thing was worrying him. If

these Japs were to be our escort he feared they would wait until they were just out of camp and then carry out our execution anyway. We were still scared for our lives, but at least a glimmer of hope was there.

Only hours to go to the court martial if things changed back, but we were the first to go on parade with fictitious names, no longer the soldiers that joined up so many years before as George Marritt and Sidney Lockwood.

All we could do was to pray for fresh guards to escort us out of Konkuita camp. I have always believed in prayer and prayed there and then. At 11.45 pm they took out the 50 men, counted them and, yes, George and I were away, cheating death by the skin of our teeth or God answering our prayers. I believe in the latter as fresh guards accompanied us on our journey to the Three Pagoda Pass.

So intense was the destruction going on all around us, that the railway line was put out of action but this didn't stop the Japs though. They brought in scores of elephants to use as another form of transportation.

These elephants were driven up over the hills and through the jungle, trampling down even more vegetation with the bulk of their size as they went, with their owner or driver, complete with his baggage strapped to the animal's back, up to where we were now working away repairing the line near to the Three Pagoda Pass.

Sledges were soon built for the elephants to pull along and these animals carted tons and tons of stores, ammunition, guns, fuel, gun carriages, wheels, anything and everything was dragged up to the front line by the elephants instead of by train, so now moving stores was the Japs' main concern.

Even these strong magnificent creatures didn't escape the Jap brutality but an elephant never forgets and really does have a good memory. As stories told in those days report that two Japs and indeed some Australians met their death by an elephant. These imposing large creatures played a very real part in our war, quiet and docile animals, intelligent and strong; they certainly took no time at all in moving what we, through frailty, now found impossible to shift.

Towards the middle of 1945 I recall all too vividly that

some of the stores were in large wooden crates and stored inside huts. The elephants couldn't be brought in close enough so POWs were used to manhandle these crates out of the huts and nearer to the waiting elephants and the handlers to lower onto the sledges.

These crates being packed with various bits of equipment, weighed about half a ton. The crates stood five feet wide and some eight feet high. Four POWs would be ordered to lift these crates up and to carry them outside, but the Jap in charge would always be on top of the crate shouting out his orders. I was one of the four on this occasion, and to my belief this day that Jap knew the war was almost lost for him. He was so determined to get his revenge that day, in so much that as we had the crate lifted up and out of the hut and about to lower it down onto the sledge, he shouted and lashed out with his split bamboo cane and hit the hands of the two POWs on the other side of the crate, causing them to let go. Down it crashed, a crate full of weighty equipment, trapping the hands of George Marritt and myself. Our hands were well and truly smashed up. We were screaming out and writhing in pain but I can still see that horrid little Japanese creature of a so-called man, jumping about on top of the crate in sheer delight like a monkey and looking down on us two completely trapped, shouting his obscenities and so pleased with himself. Our mates rushed to get crowbars to lift up the crate to release our hands but alas the damage had been done. To add to our misery further, that Jap would not allow us to go back to camp to see our medical officer for any treatment, so we had to wait until all the POWs returned to camp at the end of the days toil.

By the time we got back to camp blood was everywhere but the boys did their best with warm water. We had no ointment and the only bandages that could be found had been washed and worn a thousand times over.

At midnight a medical officer came in and asked us both how we were. He could soon see that was a stupid question on his behalf as not only had we both hands severely squashed and damaged but we had also contracted chronic malaria of the worst form. To say the least, we were both in very, very poor shape by this time.

However he attended to our hands for about four days, but when I entered his room for treatment on about day five he said "Sit down, Lockwood. You know what I'm going to say... we need to amputate your fingers as they are in such a bad state." Since my fingers were purple, frankly I didn't care at that point I just wanted to be out of pain.

There were three other POWs in the room, which just had a bench and a bamboo table. One man quickly laid on my right arm on the table, the other man pulled my left arm round behind me so I couldn't strike out and the third man lit a cigarette and said, "Shove this in your gob, it will keep you quiet for a bit" and the officer made ready for the amputation. Bear in mind I had witnessed many such surgeries when I held the mirror so I knew what fate and pain awaited me.

Mercifully, he then said he had changed his mind about amputation and started to slit open the tops of my fingers. The poison spurted everywhere and the stench was indescribable, but in so doing he slit all my fingers the same way and saved me from amputation. Much to my final relief I must add, but that was it for working days for me, for the time being anyway I thought. Little did I know we were about two weeks away from the war ending anyway. However, although my fingers mended slowly the reminders can still be seen today.

CHAPTER EIGHTEEN

MY DEDICATION TO MORT

What a man, what a friend and what a life he had...Victor

I just couldn't write this book without mentioning my very best mate Victor James Mortlock from Wickhambrook near my home town of Bury St Edmunds.

VICTOR MORTLOCK IN UNIFORM

We were both called up the same day, March 10th 1940; we

were both placed in Platoon 5, Minden Block, Gibraltar Barracks. I had never seen the man before, but there we trained together and he turned out to be a wonderful mate, a really true friend indeed in every respect. Not only did we train alongside each other, we became firm friends and went everywhere together, out and about as much as possible.

We eventually went to Holt together as mentioned earlier in the book and continued our training, even training on the carriers at the same time. Something I failed to mention earlier, we were inspected by the Prince of Wales as he was then known whilst in Holt, during the parade he noticed that my steel helmet was on, slightly at an angle. He said, "Do you know that there are only two people in the world that are allowed to wear their steel helmets on the side?"

I replied, "No, sir!"

To which the Prince of Wales said, "King Alfonso is named as one and I'm the other." I shook in my shoes, thinking this is it... doomed... on a charge no doubt... but do you know, no one said a word to me... phew! What a relief that was!

Always on a Sunday morning Mort and I would go along to the church service together. We didn't need any telling to attend church; it was an automatic process for us both, which we enjoyed. So much was our friendship that the other boys nicknamed us two "The terrible twins" because we looked so much alike, both having raven black hair and dare I boast not too bad looking either, only I was an inch taller than Victor. Mort had a peculiar walk to him, a kind of limp, but that apart he was a very nice chap. Wrote left handed, as I recall, and printed everything at that, but he would be able to print a note or letter faster than I could write normally.

So we went around Suffolk, Norfolk and on to Scotland together and it was there that the local people used to ask the battalion if they would send some boys to their guild. This meeting was held after services on a Sunday night, so you can guess who was chosen. Mort and myself being two of them!

We had some lovely times there, in the afternoon when possible, we used to go to the Red Shield in Dumfries, part of the Salvation Army, and used to always have a cup of tea and a chocolate biscuit there, just the one biscuit, mind, but believe me it was a real treat. Those people used to encourage us to bring along some mates, stating they would give them papers and pencils to write home to their parents. They used to ask us if we had in fact written home and if we said no, the reply would be "Well, you are going to do so today." This we did, doing our best to encourage more along to the meetings. These people said if we couldn't afford the stamps for our letters home, they would buy them for us. What friendship to be offered to total strangers!

From Scotland, we went down to Wales, and then we were brought back to Crewe in Cheshire. It was there that I met King George VI. He inspected our parade on one privileged occasion. We stood waiting for hours before he came along, but nevertheless we had a good visit. Previously to that momentous meeting, we had been inspected by Sir Winston Churchill. So I can lay a privileged claim to coming face to face with some very famous and valiant men during my army days.

Mort and I even managed to get embarkation leave together, eventually sailing off to Cape Town, on to Singapore and even started the fighting of the Japs alongside one another. Joined at the hip, so to speak.

As we took up our positions on the north side of Singapore island and eventually withdrew to Buka Timah cemetery, still we were in very close contact, despite all that was going on around us. It was there that Mort wanted the closer inspection of my prized watch which I have already mentioned earlier.

Remember my mentioning also his sense of humour then, which he still had later on, despite everything. Things were to rapidly change though; at four o'clock on the 15th February 1942 we were to lay down our arms and surrender. The anger welled in all the soldiers there and then. Some became very vicious at having to throw away their rifles, etc, swearing and cursing the officers giving the orders. Scuffles were soon quelled when our officers insisted we simply had no option but to surrender to the Japanese Army. From Buka Timah to Changhi, Mort and I still managed to travel together being in a party of about 50 to 60 men all from the 2nd Cambridgeshires, now effectively prisoners of war, what a dreadful feeling. Oh to have such a dear friend by your side in such dire of circumstances. It meant more than words can tell.

Then it was onto Roberts Barracks together, where we were forced-marched to the camp. Eventually we broke ranks and got a lift, passing columns of thousands and thousands of men, all marching swiftly along, very regimental and still very proud to be British, whistling as they marched. The sheer number of us was a sight to behold. We had managed to get a lift in a lorry or should I say we commandeered the lorry for ourselves, several of us together. Eventually arriving at Roberts Barracks together, we dumped the lorry which Wally Spencer had been driving and rejoined the marching ranks, many men were doing effectively the same thing as we had just done, such was the mayhem and volume of troops involved in those harrowing scenes, but amazingly we were still side by side.

Our early days at Roberts Barracks have already been covered. There, sadly and memorably for me, Mort was taken very, very ill indeed, unable to eat any of the rations provided. From there we managed to go to Siam Road Camp together. There we were sorted out into groups by the Japs, I recall Mort being well enough by then to work with me for the GPO up the telegraph posts putting up wires. Eventually we were rounded up on the tennis courts ready for the signing of the non escape papers. Still we worked alongside each other, this time boring the much-needed cess pit holes with a massive auger that the Japs brought in for us to dig out the latrine holes. About six men would pull the iron bars round and round, forcing the auger down into the ground, making the necessary and much awaited thirty-foot hole in the ground, whilst others moved away the earth that came to the surface. That freshly dug hole, which incidentally was deeper than the usual latrines around that camps, was soon put to use I can tell you. I had days and days working on such a job, we certainly could have done with more augers but, well the rest is history now, you've read about such squalor in earlier chapters.

We built the roads to the shrine together at Buka Timah and even travelled to the infamous holiday camp at Chungkai together. So much, so far and still side by side, how lucky we were given the numbers of men involved and all the tasks that pulled you this way and that, in and out of the various parties of men, all moving between dozens of camps up and down the line.

Mort and Don Dawson both succumbed to diphtheria, being such a serious illness we thought we would lose both of them there and then. Both, men along with some others, were confined to a little hut over to the side of the camp and well away from the rest of us boys. That was when the Japs used to come around and see us, some were friendly, but most, over ninety-five per cent, certainly were not, those you avoided like the plague and certainly avoided looking into their faces. If one was a little more friendly you certainly tried to latch onto him if possible to gain whatever you could. Such few as there were, these men would come to us and show us photographs of their family and ask to see any photographs we had with us.

It was then on one such friendly occasion, that I thought I would push my luck with a Jap and ask for some biscuits to eat, intended for Victor and the ill boys in the little hut and not for my consumption, mind you, as I knew the boys in the diphtheria huts were given so little if anything to eat. So I asked this Jap and made him understand what I wanted. After a couple of days, to my surprise, he found me out in the huts area, he came back to me under cover of night with two or three packets of biscuits, just what I wanted. I thanked him and he left.

When it was completely dark and all quiet, I crept out of my hut and out down the edge of the camp at about the time of the change over of the Jap guards. (I wasn't in the police force by this time, so my movements were totally forbidden.) I went down and I used to gently rattle a stick along the bamboo of their hut, so they knew it was me outside, having done this before when checking on how they were progressing and getting along. They were something pleased with the biscuits and told me all were feeling a little better by now. They enjoyed the biscuits. I'll leave you to guess what they did with the wrappers. Paper would have come in handy for a certain use, that's for sure, but they would have destroyed the evidence of my visit. I knew I could rely upon them for cover so that I didn't get caught.

However, that same Jap would very occasionally come into our hut and sit upon the end of our bed and talk to who ever happened to be with me at the time. He asked me on one such occasion was there anything else that I wanted. I said, "Yes, I want a toothbrush, please." Do you know, I never got to see that man again; I never did get the toothbrush either. Perhaps I was just being too selfish this time! What happened was they accused him of fraternising with the British prisoners, so they stopped a train load of prisoners going up the line to Burma and they put him on it and sent him up to the front line. I never saw that man again.

I then joined up with the police force and eventually managed to secure Mort a job alongside me. I also managed to get Don Dawson into the police as well, so once again all three of us were together again, both of them having recovered from their awful bout of illness. We enjoyed each other's company as best we could, going along to the concerts together and visiting church together whenever possible. It was good to be back together again at last... friends... you certainly needed them then during captivity as much as you do today.

One day Mort came along and said in a sorrowful way that he had to go up country. He said he had been picked out to go on a bridge building party. Oh dear, we had to be parted yet again. There was nothing I could do about it. They had chosen him for whatever their reasons. I was with some of the other boys from the police force and Don and myself had to reluctantly say our goodbyes to a forlorn Mort at the end of 1943 and stay behind in Chungkai... off Mort sadly went...

It was my job twice a week when the barges came down country, to go down to the river to meet the barges that were bringing the dead, sick and wounded back from further up the line. These boys would then be transferred to the Chungkai hospital, or worse still buried next day.

Now every time when I could hear the boat chugging away in the distance, I would go down to the waters edge and get myself into position to await its arrival. You could hear the Thai men on board jabbering away in their language with their light flickering in the distance, getting nearer and nearer in the darkness of night. This used to take place around midnight and there wasn't another soul around except them and me. Nobody was allowed down to the dock, only myself; that was an explicit order that had to be obeyed at all costs. Once the boat pulled in and tied up, I used to tell the Thai guards to stay right where they were. Absolutely nobody was allowed to leave the boat until I gave them authority. My orders, given to me by the Jap guards, were to be followed strictly, and you can bet your bottom dollar I was under surveillance all the time too, but from a distance.

On checking who was in command of the boat, I would get a reply such as Captain Wiseman, Royal Artillery, and then we would go through the numbers on board. Corpses first, then stretcher bearer cases, then the number of walking wounded, so a total overall would be arrived at. This would be in the region of about 70 men on board on most occasions. Maybe four or five dead soldiers, maybe up to 20 stretcher cases, and so on.

It was then my duty to double back and run to camp to the British officer in charge. The Japs would be in there in his hut with him and I'd report the numbers involved. From then on the required number of stretcher bearers would go back down to the boat with me and retrieve the corpses first; back they used to go to the respective burial place. Then they would return and bring off the stretcher cases, boys who were badly wounded and off they would set again, going to the hospital huts this time. This task alone was not easy, as the embankment of the river bed would at times be twenty to thirty feet down to the wharf and river itself. Taking place in the darkness and often in the monsoon rains, this was a treacherous task, but one which men would be only too willing to perform to help out their comrades. Carefully ensuring their casualty stayed firmly on the stretcher for fear of dropping them back and into the river. The walking wounded were the last to be allowed off the boat. They would attempt their best to scramble up this embankment and make their way back to camp, report to the British officer in charge and then be allotted to which ever hut or hospital ward could take them, and so the boats with their cargo of very frail men were emptied, under the cover of darkness.

On one particular night I saw this chap trying his best to quietly claw and crawl his way up the side of the muddy embankment and I thought to myself, good gracious that's Mort! I hadn't seen him for three months, so I asked him, "Is that you, Mort?" He didn't answer me. Still he struggled to get a foothold so I helped him up the embankment, he got a little further and I asked him again, "Is that you Mort?" Still not a word from him. He stared vacantly at me. Our bodies all looked the same in the moonlight, greyish-brown-coloured and shimmering from the humidity in the glow of the moon. Poor man, he had no strength left in his body at this point. I got him to the top of that bank, and I was still so positive in my mind that this was my best mate, that I thought I'm going to shake him hard, perhaps this poor wretched man didn't recognise me any longer, I had changed also remember. So I shook him, but gently still asked again, "Is it you Mort?"

He turned to me and cried and said, "Yes, Sid, it is me." He had recognised me at last. I now think he was so broken in spirit that he thought he would be better off dead; he didn't want his best mate to see him in this pitiful state. I asked him whatever had happened to him. He looked so bad; he replied, "They tried to kill me." Oh dear, oh dear... what a truly shocking sight to behold. I assured him not to worry and that I would look after him from there on in. I took him up to the hut where they had to go and I begged, borrowed and even stole for Mort, so much was his need of help.

He eventually got on fairly well and one evening I went along to his hut to see him again, but he cried and cried when he saw me and I asked him what was troubling him, to which he replied, "Will you get me a candle, please, Sid, because I'm afraid of the dark." Oh dear, what a sorrowful state he was mentally still in, me thinking where on earth I could get a candle from. The last line of help from a friendly Jap had long disappeared with him being sent up country, but I would somehow achieve it. I just simply had to do it for Mort.

With effort I soon found myself another reasonably sociable Jap and asked him if he could find me a candle. I managed to make him understand what it was I wanted. He came up trumps, he provided me with not one, but three candles. I paid him for them with a little spare cash I happened to have at the time. He was happy and to my knowledge kept his mouth shut. So did I...!

I took these precious candles along to Mort. He was something pleased with them. I decided to cut the candles into three parts each to give him the chance to have a little light. He appeared to get along nicely after this. Although at this point in time cholera swept through the camp and we began to lose many, many men. Not Mort...not yet!!

I still tearfully recall the nineteen mates that I did lose on one evening to this dreaded of all diseases. God rest their souls. We had become totally powerless in helping in their plight!

Eventually as time goes on and the days and weeks past, the Japs chose the "Japan parties". These parties were to be made up from the fittest of our men; they were then to be sent to Japan to work down their various mines. All men chosen were to be transported by boat. When Mort was in the sick bay very ill he said to me, "I want to go home, mate, and marry Elsie Woolard [that was his girl friend], and I want to be Post Master of Wickhambrook Post Office. I don't want my name engraved in concrete." I knew exactly what he meant. My thoughts too were echoed in his words.

One evening he told me he had been chosen to go to Japan, going on to tell me that he had been chosen to go to a better place than we were currently in. He was glad to be getting out of this dump as he put it. Mort went on to tell me the climate would be the same there as it was back home. Spring, summer, autumn and winter. I tried my best to get on the party of men to go along with him; I didn't want to say yet another goodbye. As much as I tried they wouldn't let me go.

The inevitable day came for him to parade with all these other boys that had been chosen, all to join the "Japan parties", thirty-seven of my mates' altogether, including Mort and Legge, Peacock, Spencer and many more. We all shook hands and hugged each other in our goodbyes. Mort said, "Cheerio, mate, and look after yourself. God bless you," and so we made our promises to each other and parted. We watched the parade march out of camp, as we stood in silence we waved our goodbyes, a very tearful moment then and indeed now.

That was when I found myself entirely alone but of course I wasn't alone, the Dear Lord was still with me and I would soon make friends with other men again, but how I missed them all, there was such a void of emptiness and lack of familiar faces and voices for a while.

At the time they departed it would be about May of 1944. Some two to three months later, towards the end of July, we were on parade one evening when the Jap interpreter came up to the rostrum and shouted to us English b`s to be quiet and shut up. He proceeded to read all these 200 names out to us, going on to say that we wouldn't be seeing any of them again as they had all been drowned, and concluded his frank announcement by stating they had been sunk by our friends in the American submarine boats.

Mort's name, along with all my friends' names, had been called out from his list. It was numbing, so cold and calculated. Imagine how I and many other men felt. At that particular time on parade, you could hear and feel the stunned silence, you could have heard a pin drop in the dust of that camp floor, and every one was totally silent. As soon as the Jap gave the dismiss things rapidly changed, the prisoners of war called the guards everything under the sun. You never heard such language in all your life.

What they were going to do to them all, all of which they truly deserved. Well that was the last I was to hear of Mort and my other friends, assuming they had all drowned on the Japanese boat party that had left weeks earlier. Incidentally there were eleven such boats in that infamous Japan boat convoy. Some historians have written about this disaster and film coverage has been made.

I will tell you about the ending of the war for me later, but to conclude this dedication to Mort, as I never saw him again, it was way after my homecoming, some few years later that I learned the horrible truth of his death. Much to my relief some of those thirty-seven men did miraculously survive and I'm in touch with several today but as for Mort...?

I visited Willy Peacock with my family at his home. It took some time to trace Willy and his whereabouts. He was and is still living on a smallholding in the Fens in Cambridgeshire, and he, immediately on our arrival, said to me, "I know what you've come to ask me about, Sid, what happened to Mort," and he told us that Mort wasn't drowned but he was suffocated to his death. I couldn't believe his words. I stood motionless for a moment or two, unable to comprehend. We didn't discuss things about Mort any further during that visit, we couldn't. I felt absolutely sure no one could suffocate my best mate. This comment stuck in my mind for several more years. It might seem hard for the reader to understand after the war, that although conversations struck up about our captivity, it was often too painful to recall and some conversations were never concluded, including this one with Willy and me talking about Mort.

By chance at one of our reunion meetings that I began to attend in my home town in my latter years, I heard two or three boys, now elderly pensioners like myself, talking together about the Japan boat party. You see, some of them did escape with their lives thankfully, Legge, Spencer, Peacock, etc, but not Mort. So I went over to the men at the meeting and said, "Excuse me, but were you on the Japan party yourselves?" to which they confirmed they indeed were. So not all the men had died as we were told back in those awful days in camp by that wretched Jap interpreter. Clearly he had lied.

Naturally I went on to ask them if they knew of a man called Victor Mortlock. I relayed my version of events and went on to confirm that he had been suffocated to death, which I could not believe. Promptly one gentleman said, "You can believe it mate and I'll tell you how it was done."

He went on to say that the first thirty POWs aboard were pushed down into the holds of those eleven boats. They went down by rope step ladder into the hold. These men were then forced and turned to go into little cages feet first. A Jap guard stood there with a bayonet and rammed them in. The bloke who told me all this story stated they could not possibly live down there because of the sheer stifling heat in that hold. This gentleman turned to the other person at our meeting and said he saw them go in there so he knew it to be true; he was quite emphatic and precise about the details. To which he was, even all these years later, challenged as to why he hadn't been put into such a cage himself. He swiftly replied stating he was too sharp for them and went back up that ladder as fast as his legs would carry him, three times quicker than he had descended the rope ladder. What he saw must have scared him stiff. He then hid himself away by diving under a tarpaulin, covering up steel pipes which were on route back to Japan. That swift action saved his life. Another man who had been listening to us talking and taking in this conversation at the meeting opened up and said he too did the self-same thing; thus both avoided suffocation. So the truth was now emerging at last. All these decades later I was to learn of the chilling truth of Mort's death.

I will withhold the names of the three comrades involved at that reunion meeting to protect their families but they are still friends of mine today and I can bear witness to them relaying this awful truth. In many ways I was glad, yet obviously very saddened, to get somewhere nearer to the truth and to hear their news but at least I could come to terms with how Mort died. But... they went on to tell us all something else. Those eleven boats laid off Singapore, close to Changhi for three weeks, so their journey to Japan really never took place as the voyage was severely delayed, delayed long enough for many deaths to occur.

They lay off the main Singapore Harbour, nearby to Changhi Camp but unable to set sail to sea because of the intense and ferocious submarine activity going on there at the time. They confirmed the boats sat there for three weeks solid in stifling hot days, yes, suffocating heat. These men at our meeting went on to confirm that during the nights of those three weeks, those fit enough had to bring up the dead from down in the holds and throw them overboard, just like a bag of rubbish dumped into the Pacific Ocean. My guess is if Mort went to his death in such a way, that someone would have taken his watch off him.

Men were in such a terrible state they didn't really care what happened to them or what they did to others. No doubt those in the little cages down in the holds perished, but the Japs would have insisted that the cages would soon be reoccupied once again. Only until the next night, no doubt, when the next occupant too would have been dumped overboard, and so this atrocity went on with those eleven boats for three weeks.

Eventually the convoy did in fact set sail for Japan and Willy can tell you how far they got, before they too were all torpedoed. Willy has since concluded this story for me and verified things by saying that he managed to cling perilously to some wreckage at sea for about forty-eight hours. He told me that what the Japs did after that was unthinkable really. They had already inflicted so much torture and death on this boat party. But he went on to tell me, if the Japs were close enough in their boats to some survivors in the water, they would prod them with long poles and hold the prisoners' heads under water with the poles until they drowned the POWs. Willy saw this going on with his own eyes, along with a couple or so other prisoners that also were clinging to his wreckage. Miraculously they managed to avoid this affliction. In a couple of days the Japs sent their destroyers through the wreckage scene, where men were still trying to survive amongst the dead bodies. These destroyers had long ropes attached to them, so if you were lucky enough and strong enough and indeed quick enough to grasp hold of the rope you did, Willy was such a man. Quite determined by now that nothing would finish him off at this stage, so eventually he managed to haul himself up and onto the destroyer and was saved.

So... sadly that is where I have to end this tribute to my dear friend. Knowing of his sad departing did not ease my pain, only confirmed to me the horrors of this awful war. Taking and claiming many good men, I can only conclude he did not die in vain. He too was fighting for his King and Country; "those that grow not old, age shall not weary them, nor do the years condemn." I will remember this dear man Mort until my dying day and am truly grateful to have had him beside me, through so many years of hardship and counted him as my dearest friend... may his soul rest in God's peace.

VICTOR MORTLOCK ON LEAVE

CHAPTER NINETEEN

AFTER OUR RELEASE

Now for the rest of my story. Back at the Three Pagoda Pass near to Konkuita, we were possibly amongst the last of the camps to realise that the war had ended, being up the furthest end of the line so to speak. This may sound unbelievable but up until this point we had no idea whatsoever of how the war was actually going on. We knew nothing at the time of the atom bombs or bombings that we taking place elsewhere, other than those that had been landing on our parts of the railway line.

I had already had my hands both severely damaged, plus a really bad case of malaria at Konkuita, so I was effectively too ill to go on to the line to work. Things were really a total blur to me now and I really did think my time was now to be very short indeed. How much longer could I hold on? My guess was at weeks rather than months by this stage.

But were hostilities about to be ended at last? Strangely enough, we were hustled out of our huts one night by the Japs still brandishing their bayonets, believe it or not. They sharply told us to get out and take the sick men with us and take the train to Singapore. At last a chance to escape hoping they wouldn't shoot us all there and then and make use of those deep ditches around us. So this was liberation? We weren't sure even now, nor would anybody think it was over with a bayonet still in their face.

Did we take all the sick and wounded men with us? I fear not. We made such a speedy exit from that camp, as fast as our little bodies would allow us. We would have numbered less that 200 at this point, I think, that is all that had managed to survive out of the hundreds that had entered Konkuita camp. It was a close call, wasn't it, but at last I was moving outward and hopefully homeward, but I wasn't really sure what was happening, to be honest; activity all around was more than a blur.

I recall how we were to be moved down line some two hundred and twenty miles towards Chungkai, then past that old camp and on further. We travelled in open rail trucks this time. Whether the journey took one night or two I cannot recall. I felt pretty rough by this time, I can tell you. What I can vividly recall is that many men were arm in arm on leaving the huts, physically helping each other along to the trucks. This one poor man, in a very poor state of health said, "Leave me here to die, I'm too weak to travel with you."

I replied, "No way, I'm blowed if I'm going to leave you here now. We've come this far and survived, we can get you home somehow, I know that much."

We had left enough dear departed friends behind in the cemeteries as it was, many freshly dug graves etched in our minds, many still right within our view so we were not prepared to leave any more, not now.

With that George and me rolled the poor man on to the ground and proceeded to drag him along on his backside and his heels. We both dragged him as gently as we could, but also as quickly as we could, down to where the trucks were waiting for us. Then we thought how would we get him on board, there was no door. We had to all clamber on board and over the sides of the steel truck the best we could. He couldn't; this poor man had all but had it. So thinking quickly how we could manage this task, we had no ladder and no platform to use, I suggested that I would climb on board the truck nearest to the engine, using the train's bolts and chains to pull me up and over the sides, then drop over inside the truck, then asked the other men to throw over what belongings they had with them, so that I could make a kind of makeshift platform on the inside of the truck to stand upon and lean back over the outside of the wagon to reach down to grab this poor man.

My hands, still fully bandaged didn't make this task easy but however, the POWs then hoisted this poor man up as far as they could manage to lift him, I leant over with what little strength I had, as far as I could, my stomach on the edge of the side of the truck and my leg supporting me on the inside, and on the command they pushed and heaved the man up towards me. I was able to grab hold of his hands, so that I could pull him upwards. With one almighty heave, he landed and was lodged up beside me on the edge of the truck. There the two of us looked at each other, stranded, stuck in fact, him not quite knowing what to do. I thought I can't hold him, and I can't let him go, or otherwise he will drop back and crash down to the ground and that will be the end of that! The fall would kill him. So I remember putting my left leg up on the inside of the truck wall and with one almighty huge pull, I literally had to yank him over the side and down onto the inside of the truck floor itself. He came hurtling down with one hefty thump, like a sack of coal, fortunately missing me as well, but tumbling on the inside and landing somehow on the make shift piles below. I use the word hefty but you can imagine none of us weighed more than five or six stones.

By that time one or two of the other chaps had clambered in and made it over the side, so we made old matey as comfortable as we could, propped up against George and myself in a corner for the rest of the journey. At least he was away from that awful camp near Konkuita and on his way to freedom. One less victim to be claimed by that formidable jungle.

This was around midnight by now, there were no Japs around, they had gone, for the first time in well over three and a half long years we were unguarded, that in itself was overwhelming.

We had just left the Three Pagoda Pass area and had to travel about two hundred or more miles back to Ban Pong, really as far as the line went from one end to the other. This time we were transported in open coal trucks and not those dreaded enclosed steel trucks we had used some three and a half years earlier. The necessary toilet stops were made and those able climbed in and out for the call of nature. Several men had to still defecate where they were, unable to exit the truck due to sheer fatigue and weariness.

On one of these stops, I did what I badly needed to do and then as I went to get back aboard the train, I thought, what on earth is that standing there? It was like a vision, a mirage looming by the track, quivering in the intense heat. I couldn't see that clearly, actually, and had no real idea of what I was looking at; it was shimmering away in the heat and not at all clear. What it turned out to be was a local native, selling two baskets of fruit. Somebody went up to him and bang wallop, down he went and out for the count. All of his fruit was quickly stolen, I stole some, one banana in fact, such was my desperation. I couldn't see him at first, but I could see a banana lying on the ground. I reckon that those two baskets of fruit vanished in five seconds flat; we were ravenous. We were still hungry and desperate men, just under two hundred of us, plainly ravenously hungry and starving men, judging by what we had just done to this poor native. Had no food, got no food. I felt rather sorry after I'd done it, thinking what on earth have I come to now, still stealing. The old engine driver kept on whistling for us all to get back on board. This we did and off we set again, leaving the old man lying beside the tracks.

Travelling back through and past the very areas where we had rigorously worked as prisoners. Seeing the sides of the embankment we had built up, knowing full well we were travelling over our dear dead departed friends and comrades that we were made to bury beneath the line. On past the many, many cemeteries, some with crosses still visible, some overgrown with time, but all too full of our men.

Mournfully we left many, many hundreds of dead soldiers behind us. It turned out to be thousands and thousands in the very end. Thinking ahead now of being reunited with our loved ones, but it was hard; we couldn't help but spare our thoughts for those who were not as fortunate as us to survive this dreadful war. Being held prisoners with us in its many prison camps along the line, only to lose their personal fight for life itself.

At this point I recall I weighed in at six stone eight pounds, having left my parents' home all those years earlier weighing ten stone ten pounds. It was questionable as to whether I and many others were yet fit enough for the journey home.

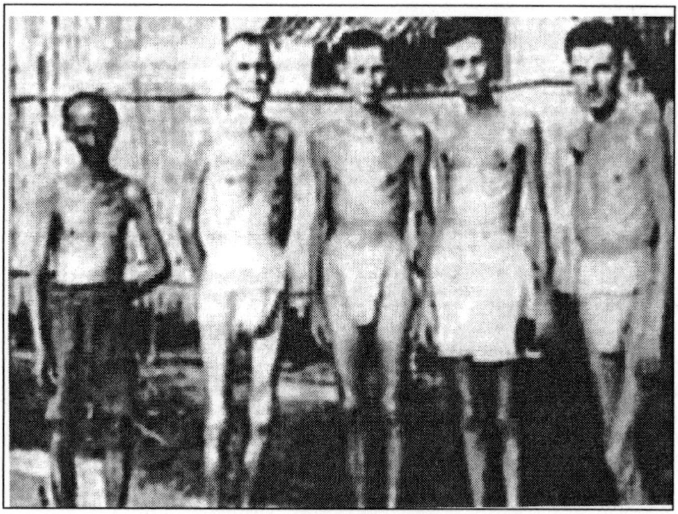

PICTURE OF SOME OF THE P.O.W.s

It was coming over one of the many bridges that I really felt bad. I looked down from the Wangpo bridge, as it snaked around the hillside, the line itself appearing to be clinging for its very existence to the rock face on the one side and overhanging the deep gorge below us on the other side. We were only travelling about 5 mph. The train was just creeping along but you could hear the many creaks and loud bangs as the trucks rolled on over the thousands of sleepers laid by the POWs. Hundreds of men lost their lives building this hugely tall construction. It was all wooden. I said to George, "Look at that sight."

George said, "I daren't look, I daren't look." I continued sheepishly looking over the edge of our wagon and hoping the boys in our truck didn't attempt to do the same and all come over to one side to take a look, fearing it would topple the entire train with its truckloads of men completely over the edge. Death was still only a stone's throw away even now!

Little did we contemplate whilst travelling over this bridge at the time, what might have happened all those months and indeed years earlier. As the bridge construction was built, I'm sure to this day, that as much by way of sabotage that could be done would have been effectively done. Anything would have certainly been attempted by the prisoners to thwart the Japanese from completing their tasks, and here we were, all riding high on this construction taking in the awesome sights on our homeward journey.

TRAVELLING HOMEWARD

The Mekong River came at us in the one direction and the River Kwai in the other. They eventually crossed each other, so to speak. It was at this corner, near by the rivers meeting, that our train finally came to rest in a cutting. It was on arrival at the station that we were met by some big British guys, or should I say they looked big to us compared against our slight skeletons. Well would you credit it; they started to bellow and shout at us, just like the Japs we had left behind had treated us.

Was our war over? Out of about the two hundred so-called fit men able to commence that train journey from Konkuita, only about one hundred stood there at the station. The others were too ill to dismount from the trucks, or sadder still many lost their lives and died on that fateful journey homeward and still lay behind us where they had died on the truck floor in front of our eyes, we being powerless to help in any way whatsoever. So near and yet so far from freedom, theirs was only the freedom of pain and starvation.

The British troops had provided pails and pails of hard boiled eggs. They were everywhere and we were to be encouraged to help ourselves. What you must bear in mind at this point is, we just could not eat them at all, having only seen rice for years. So to enable us to stomach these eggs daily, they said they would build the ration up slowly. Two daily with biscuits and so forth until we were consuming the required amount of eight eggs a day. For the first time in years we were soon going to be able to sip on a real cup of tea, complete with sugar and milk which was not included in our so-called boiled tea up on the line. Mouth-watering news, our need was still desperate we were parched dry but tea... that wasn't to be... not just yet anyway!!

The reason being that this jumped-up regimental sergeant major climbed high up onto an atap hut, so that he could see us, and started to shout at us all. Loudly blurting out like some lunatic that the war was over. Telling us the Japs had surrendered on the 15th August 1945, unbelievably some two or three weeks earlier, and this was how we were to be informed. So from March 10th 1940 when I first signed up until now, this was what we had been fighting for, a loud mouthed RSM that had no respect whatsoever for what or who stood before him. Or for what state of health we were in, or for those departed souls still lying in the trucks behind us. Those five and a half years flashed through my brain with a blink of an eyelid. Was I going mad, had I gone mad when I saw the mirage earlier with the old man with his basket of desperately needed fruit, or had I dreamt all this wretched prisoner of war captivity up? My head was simply reeling.

Believe me or not, he called us POWs everything under the sun that he could lay his tongue to. His attitude alone was totally shameful, not to mention his language. There was us, barely able to stand or walk, some of the two hundred that started out on this train journey had not even survived their last homeward journey and died en route, still lying in the trucks behind us. Most of us almost naked with no clothing, we looked filthy dirty, withered and worn away through the ravages we had endured from the Japs, and now our own men were showing us no mercy whatsoever. Who could we turn to? The RSM went on to state that he would knock a lot of discipline into us blokes. He f'd and blinded at us and went ahead alarmingly. He was just unbelievable. I thought I was going to go completely mad, my head banged inside my skull. The war was over I wanted to celebrate, I was free, but from what?

That was enough for us. With what little strength we did have left, we took to our heels without any encouragement from each other, and just fled, running as fast as our little legs would carry us off into the jungle and hid. Scared absolutely stiff again, this time by our own men, mentally we couldn't handle any more!

We were older and somewhat wiser now but nevertheless we were frightened blokes and we simply scattered everywhere, just like sheep, such was the state of our minds; it was sorrowful.

George and me and two blokes from Beds and Herts group lay together, hidden up in the dense shrubbery. All the trees around had been felled long ago. So us four huddled together fearful of what was about to happen to us. On the way into our hideaway, we saw some pails full of eggs, so we each whipped some as we passed. We thought we'd be gone long enough to have a meal or two, I guess. Hoping silently that they would leave us alone, but that in truth would have finished us off completely, with hindsight.

The British troops were still trying to get us all back together, but we were having nothing of it, we just scampered and went further and deeper into the jungle, but they didn't pursue this time, they didn't come for us.

We lay hidden away all night and several hours went by. We found we couldn't stomach those eggs, by the way. So there we lay, a cloudy night, war over, released, still in our little jock straps, feeling rough, but this time hiding from the English army. How bizarre could things get? I suppose it proved how near to madness we had all become.

Dawn came and still we hid up, when at around 6am a Canadian military paratrooper came into the jungle and found us. He was a little bloke. He stumbled across the four of us in our hideaway and said, "Come on, I'm not going to hurt any of you. That was the worst thing the RSM could have done, to shout, swear and curse at you men as he did." He carried on to say that he wanted us all to leave with him and go back out into the open. We all hesitated for a long while, before we decided to go with him. George and I agreed we might as well go out with him. This would be about 8am by now.

So the Canadian ushered the four of us out of our jungle hideaway and took us along to some wash places. There were four areas already rigged up with a shower of a sort, surrounded by hessian sackcloth for privacy. This was a new one on us, for the last few years we had spared each other no dignified washing facilities. You just bathed were you could and if you could, onlookers and all. There was no modesty further up that line, but in truth mostly back up the line we stayed dirty, too tired to make the trip down to the water's edge whilst in camp.

We were told to go into the shower, one into each cubicle. I soon got into one, the others taking up their places too. As we entered these prepared areas, he told us to take a pail full of cold water and a pail full of hot water with us into the cubicle. The next thing I knew this man was on his hands and knees, when he pitched me under the hessian cloth a bar of soap!! He said, "Scrub your blinking self really clean." I got hold of the bar of soap in amazement and came hurriedly out of the cubicle and went in to see George with this treat. Soap! We hadn't seen soap for nearly four years. I was so excited to even hold the bar, let alone have a wash with it. I went straight into George's cubicle with me blabbing out, "Look George, I've got a bar of soap!"

George grinned and replied "Cor! ... you know what we'd have done with that a few weeks back, Sid." and we both agreed we would have eaten it. That's for sure, we would have, too!

So I came back out and into my own little shower cubicle again, gladly got out of my ragged and dirty jock nappy and had the first real good scrub I'd had in years. It seemed to take me ages. The mud was caked on my body but I couldn't manage to get around to washing my own back. My hands were still bandaged up from the injury so that made things difficult for a start, but the truth was I was almost exhausted with scrubbing the filth off, that I hadn't even got the energy to complete this simplest of human personal tasks. So off I set again and went back in with George and asked him to scrub my back, then I would scrub his. The other two blokes were doing the same thing. We ended up having to have another couple of pails of water to get really somewhere towards being clean, as we were absolutely caked-in, utter dried-on, cracked mud and filth. The Canadian kept with us all the time to make sure we did as instructed, checking progress was to his required standard. He then pitched us in a towel each. Another luxury I hadn't seen for years, now a towel of our own to dry with. Civilisation was hopefully about to return to our lives. We dried and wiped ourselves all down, and then he gave us a pair of clean trunks to put on. What a carry-on, but what a wonderful treat, clean and better clothed at last.

Now perhaps my family might recognize me when I see them again. I'm somewhat better dressed, I'm thin, I'm black in colour, I'm gaunt, I'm looking half crazed but miraculously I'm still alive, thank God.

The Canadian then took us along to an area where there sat eight officers. We, along with others by now, all stood in line, waiting to go up to each officer at his desk in turn. The first officer said to me, "You don't know who you are, do you?"

To which I replied, "Yes I do" and went on to quote my name, rank and number.

He then went on to say to me, "Well, you don't know who your next of kin are, do you?"

To which I replied, "Yes I do" and went on to tell him of my parents' names.

He then went on to question me further and said, "Well you don't remember where you live, do you?"

To which I replied, "Of course I do" and related to him my family address.

Being satisfied I was still coherent I was asked to move along to the next officer, but you can clearly see now how crazed and mad we must have looked, it was right of them to question us in such a way due to our appearance alone, I guess.

The second officer looked at me and said, "We're going to take some blood from you, rather a lot of blood." So as a result of the blood test being taken, they couldn't tell us what was going to happen until 8am the next morning when the results would be through. So we were warned that we might not be going home just yet. We had to wait longer to see the outcome of the tests.

Then on to the third officer. He offered me three tablets and told me to take them with some water from the jug using the mug on his table. So doing as I'm told, I duly swallowed the prescribed medication then onwards again to the fourth man.

The fourth officer was an officer in the medical corps. He said, "Hello what's the matter here?" He was looking down at my bandaged fingers. He swiftly took hold of his scissors and cut off the old rags. "God blimey, chap," he said. He was flabbergasted at the sight of them. "What a hand to take home to your mother," he said. The officer went on to say that he would have to amputate my fingers. One of the other officers debated with him and stated that he couldn't amputate there and then because they had nothing available to do it with. So this was the second time my fingers had been threatened with amputation. Between them it was decided that I had to wait until I reached Rangoon and then the operation would be performed. In the meanwhile they said that they had to hurt me further, by painting my hands with iodine liquid, but that was nothing to what I had already been through. My fingers were dressed and I was re-bandaged, with clean ones for a change. The least I could hope for was that anaesthetic would be readily available at Rangoon, still recalling all too vividly the screams from the men I had helped through such previous unaided amputation operations up in the jungle camps.

On to the fifth officer who gave me some more clothes. I recall a vest. I was then able to have my chest and back covered for the first time in years. Can you imagine such basic things being so welcomed back into your life? He went on to give me two hard boiled eggs and a cup of tea and a small packet of biscuits. Same with George; we were still side by side in the queue, so to speak, passing from table to table, officer to officer. Then we were told to go and sit down nearby to eat and drink like civilised human beings. For the first time in what now seemed like an eternity we were now beginning to act a bit more normally.

We passed on through the other officers for whatever reason I now cannot state, but we knew that we had to return the following morning for the results of the blood tests. Before that my brief was to return at 5.30 pm that evening to have my hand redressed. The same thing was happening to George as our injuries were identical, having both been crushed at the same time by the falling crate.

Where I slept that night eludes me now, but I recall going back in the morning for the blood results. The officer looked at me and said, "Lockwood, you are too weak to move out yet. We cannot fly you out as your blood count is dangerously low." News I didn't want to hear, of course. He went on to state that he didn't know what he was going to do with me yet, going on to suggest to me that I eat as many as eight eggs a day. So it was to be, that I remained there at a hospital area for ten long further days recuperation to try to build up my strength, which now with hindsight I clearly needed, eggs and all.

Finally I was passed fit enough to travel, along with George and others who were fit enough to move. We were told to make our way to Bangkok. I therefore asked how I was to travel... that officer's reply was, "Find your own way"... just like that!! George and I commented that we must have to walk it then, knowing it was some sixty miles away.

We started to walk on towards the Mekong River, which we had to cross first before making the long hike to Bangkok. That was our first worry; how would we get across this huge river? When we arrived at the edge of the waters we found that it was all arranged for us. Boats tied up there could be used by the POWs, six of us at a time got in with the Thai man in charge of the boat. Ropes had been attached to the remains of an old bridge on the far shore, which had been bombed and rendered useless. So we all proceeded to haul and drag ourselves across by these ropes, effectively crossing the Mekong River. That Thai man would then drag himself back empty for a repeat journey and another load of fellow ex-POW men.

When we reached the other side of the river, well you never see so much filth in all your life, it was nearly as bad as back up in the camps. Up to our knees in sewage yet again, so much for that wonderful wash ten days ago. We could use another pail or two of water right now but we were heading homeward so what the heck! We had to wade several yards through this muck to reach dry land a bit further along. Some local natives were still trying to sell their wares even now, so anyone that had a little cash on them could buy whatever, fruit and eggs etc. I had no cash at all.

We got through the mire and onto the road. There we saw a lorry standing waiting complete with its driver. I said to George, "Look there's a lorry, let's take it."

The Indian driver on board hadn't a clue what was about to happen to him. I was so determined that he wasn't going to drive the thing. I wanted that lorry for myself. I could see this as my vehicle of escape at last! So I went after him and tried to pull him out of the cab, with what little strength I could muster, having used most up on the ropes crossing the Mekong River. The Indian put his parts on, so did I. I kept on trying to dislodge him from his seat, shoving and pushing him around and calling him everything I could think of, so to speak. The blokes on the back of the lorry told George to give me a fourpenny one... clout on the chin in other words, to knock me out. I'd gone somewhat demented, crazed, and desperate to commandeer this vehicle; nothing was going to stop me driving this lorry to Bangkok. My mates could see I had gone more or less half crazy. I was abruptly stopped... somebody gave me such a wallop that I came round on the back floor of the lorry, having been ceremoniously dumped there like a sack of potatoes by some of my so-called mates. Well in truth and with hindsight, they did the correct thing at the time; I had to be stopped no matter what as I had no control of my emotions whatsoever, or indeed of what I was doing at the time.

Eventually on my feet again and somewhat calmer by now, all the men on board the lorry stood up for the journey to Bangkok. It was fully loaded. You could get thirty or more of us skinny blokes on board standing, but it would have been less in numbers if we had sat down for the duration of the journey. Many thousands of men were now desperate to return to their native homeland and families. So our sixty mile journey was about to get under way again, standing this time, packed in that lorry like sardines. By the way I still didn't have any shoes at this time. I must have got those at our next destination... Bangkok.

So much was the load of men; the Indian driver didn't get the lorry out of second gear for a very long while. Strange thing to recall but once a driver, always a driver. From meat delivery van back home, to Bren gun carrier, to an American six-wheel-drive lorry and now this lorry, wearily trudging and pulling us, its cargo of ex-POWs all homeward. Perhaps he thought his beleaguered cargo was so fragile he had better take it steady, who knows? Perhaps I thought I could make a better job of driving the lorry than him; doubt it though, not at that period in time, any rate!

We had actually been released about two weeks or so by this time and we were now travelling from Ban Pong to Bangkok, where the whole wretched episode in our lives came to a so-called end. Here we now were, thousands of strange-looking Englishmen and many others, travelling along in lorries back to Bangkok. The journey seemed endless, our legs and bodies ached, but we were to safely arrive later that evening.

What a sight was unfolding before our eyes, men appearing from everywhere. Every nationality under the sun represented there on the roads leading from Ban Pong. All in degrading states of health and mind, we now somewhat better dressed in clothes provided by the British Army for our homeward journey, still shoeless but what the heck... penniless too, but free men at last.

We were being driven along in these lorries, when I could not believe my own eyes. There in amongst the throng of hundreds and hundreds of refugees moving slowly along was Mr Bull. He too was also en route to Bangkok, having left his little kampong way behind in the jungle outside Chungkai. He had changed somewhat too. Straightaway I recognized him as we were edging our way through with the lorry. He was jabbering away to himself, which was a trademark of this remarkable man.

I immediately jumped up with George and clambered down from the back of the lorry. We all embraced each other, long and hard. His eyes lit up as he was hugging me, I naturally asked of him and his family but he replied, "No good, no good."

I looked around him whilst we were being jostled along by

the crowds of people, to see if I could see his family especially little Sammy, but he was all alone. I asked, "Where is Sammy, then?"

To which he replied, "You no heard?" Explaining to him that after our last encounter I had been moved further up the line towards Burma, so I had no idea what he was about to tell me. He carried on to say, "Sammy in paradise." I obviously questioned him, unbelievingly further, to find out that two Jap lorries had been used to crush Sammy to his death. They each backed up onto him, crushing him between the rear of the two vehicles, simply because the lad knew too much, having spent some time in and around the camps up the line.

We sadly moved on with the throng of people pressing against us. I had nothing in the world to give Mr Bull, neither had George. We walked together for about a mile then he pushed us forward and gently said, "You go home to England."

George and I realised there was nothing we could do. We bade him a very fond farewell, watched him go on amidst the jostling crowds of people, quickly losing sight again then we jumped aboard the next lorry that passed, making its way to Bangkok aerodrome for our flight out to Rangoon.

What fond memories I still carry today of that incredible man and his family. Oh! to be able to locate him and hear of his story, what a story that would be, but my guess is he is already in the glory land. What a miracle that encounter turned out to be, from all those thousands of men and women making their way down that road, amongst all the vehicles travelling down the dusty streets, that Mr Bull should stand out in the crowd. That just sums up this marvellous man; he simply stood up and stood out, head and shoulders above the rest of us for his acts of bravery and kindness. All of which he freely showed in a humble and selfless way towards us starving POWs in the camps. Strangers in his homeland whom he treated like his brothers.

On arrival at Bangkok aerodrome, there were loads of tents and huts ready and waiting for us to all use. These blocks of accommodation had been used beforehand by the many hundreds and hundreds of men whom had arrived earlier. They had been processed in and out and were on their way home already. We arriving later having made a considerably longer journey down to Bangkok were now to be processed in exactly the same manner as men before us.

The officers in charge at Bangkok had food and water in abundance for us to partake of, but still our stomachs were not acclimatised to such luxury, well at least not much of it, anyway. I recall spending just the one night at the aerodrome and then we were to be airlifted out in groups of twenty-five men and flown to Rangoon aerodrome. This is where I must have been given my pair of shoes. You would have thought I would be able to recall exactly about this item of apparel, having spent many years barefoot working on the railway, but the details escape me now.

George and I were still accompanying each other around and we were due to be flown out at noon the next day. So we joined our comrades in a group of the required twenty-five men and made our way out on the runway to the awaiting plane. I believe it was a Lancaster but I'm not too sure. We climbed aboard this aeroplane to be greeted by four or five medical officers.

It was their job to chaperone us on all of the journey to Rangoon, looking after our safety and above all our health. We were instructed to sit on the floor of the plane the best we could. Not that our belongings took up any space, we had nothing, no full kit bags, no presents for the families from our so-called holiday camp, nothing... except what we stood up in.

It was an empty shell of a plane for the purpose of transporting us up country to Rangoon. There was us, having been through what we had, survived the rigours of the jungle and all it could throw at us, lived with those tormenting captors of Jap guards and believe it or not, we were now stupidly asking for parachutes, in case the worst happened, how futile was that? The officers soon assured us we would be quite safe, if we felt any air sickness we were to call to an officer for assistance. They could see what kind of a state we were all still in emotionally and physically. Men still needing the toilet quickly and some even passing out at this experience of having to fly. Men still in bandages, on crutches, skeletonised human beings, hobbling amputees, but still all very proud men indeed, still soldiers at heart. Sixty years on it is all still so vivid, so you can only imagine what thoughts controlled our mind and bodies in those very early days of release. You could say we were still scared stiff, unable to comprehend the changes that were happening to us.

We were all safely loaded aboard, apprehensive of the six hundred mile journey ahead, which was to take up to six hours. Up the plane engines roared and we started to roll down the runway. As we slowly lifted off away from those camps of hell I remember taking a brief look out of the window and looking down below, I caught sight of the last Japanese soldier I was to see. He was parading around the end of one of the huts below us. On reflection I don't know what I thought at the time. Did I hate those men for what they had done to me? I cannot really say that I hated them. They were forced to do what they did for the most part. That was to be my last sighting and glimpse of those horrible days of captivity, that was, until the pilot of the aircraft spoke to us all on the tannoy.

The pilot told us he was going to fly us down low, over the track of the rivers and be flying along the railway line we had just built. We all peered bleary-eyed out of the windows, anxious to see for ourselves. We could see the clearings, the many cuttings we had forged and all the camps we had built below us. The very line itself, winding its way along the jungle floor, and the thousands of sleepers along the way, plus unused piles of bamboo still stacked at the sides of the tracks. There was a deathly hush aboard that plane, a numbing sight unfolded, and the reality of working so hard down there flooded back. The noises, the smells, the sights, the illnesses, the friendships, the desperation for food and even death itself, were all quickly racing through my brain. Emotions ran high, tears flowed from many a man.

What of the many mens' grave below us, sadly men never able to return home, what would happen to their graves... I don't know how I felt... I don't know what I thought...I was just so glad to be flying up and away from it all. Chaps were gradually chatting a little more by now; some still felt too emotional and unwell even by this stage to speak, the flight itself not helping, I suspect, but all of us had an overwhelming sense of relief slowly filtering back into our beleaguered lives.

We touched down at Rangoon; actually it was a little aerodrome just outside Rangoon. The total relief at the end of this journey was just simply immense. All the twenty-five soldiers on board this plane firmly shook the hands of the pilots and the medical officers, so hard you'd have thought we would have broken their wrists; such was our relief and gratitude for that flight of mercy to our freedom. It was not to be such a lucky flight for three other planeloads of POWs; they crashed for whatever reason and men perished along with their pilots. We were the lucky ones this time around, but we didn't know of these reports until some time later.

Old Austin ambulances were there to meet us as we alighted from the plane. Some men were still stretcher cases unable to walk. We were so small you could have got about four men onto a stretcher at one time, I would reckon. I was lucky enough to be amongst the walking wounded, hands still heavily bandaged as was George, so the both of us made our way back to the control area for yet more processing.

We were quickly dispatched to Rangoon Hospital. All these beds were awaiting us, proper beds, a mattress, pillow and lovely clean white bed sheets. What a sight, I was the first to jump onto mine, I lumped down so hard it's a wonder I didn't break the thing. I was just so pleased to see a normal bed at last, a far, far cry from the slats of bamboo we had used as our resting place at nights.

More injections were to follow, pills and medication we nearly died for a few days earlier. All now freely available to us. Medication was probably around all the time back up the line somewhere previously, but the Japs would not hear of us being allowed anything. There we both lay for eleven days in Rangoon hospital recuperating. We must have been given a hair cut somewhere back on this journey, I was so ill I don't even recall that occurrence. I must also have been reunited with a toothbrush too. Normal life was returning; everybody was trying so hard for us, too.

About seven days into this stay of recuperation, the orderlies said that we had got to try and get out of the hospital and go for little walks to help build up our strength. They advised us to attempt to go down into the town and have a look around. Off George and I strolled. We came to this imposing building, unsure of what it was, so we proceeded to go up and inside. George said, "Look at all those steps, Sid, how do you fancy your chances going up them?" We both agreed to try and make it to the top, so off we set to go inside this building. Well what a shock... up at the top we were told to take our shoes off. We couldn't make this out, how strange, what was behind those doors for me to have to take off my much prized shoes? I'd been years without any, now I'm being told to take them off again. How strange was this foreign land!

Shoeless again, when we looked inside it was a Buddhist temple. I was totally amazed. There was a great big golden idol sitting in there. I said to George, "Come on, George, let's get out of here real quick." I've never put a pair of shoes on as quickly as that since, off down those steps we trotted, no, ran as quickly as we could. Out and away from their graven image. That really was the last thing I was expecting to find inside. Naiveté even then at their religious beliefs. With hindsight, I suppose the graven image I saw, was frightening to me! Our minds were somewhat twisted by the Japanese culture that we had just been released from. In my state-of-mind I could not handle what I saw.

Whilst we were in Rangoon Hospital, after about the first four days or so of complete rest, George and I would be allowed to take it in turns to go down to the post room to collect the mail for each other. It made a welcome change to stretch your legs and go for a walk along the corridors, past the other men seeing all the sights, chatting with friends and catching up on how they were progressing with their ailments.

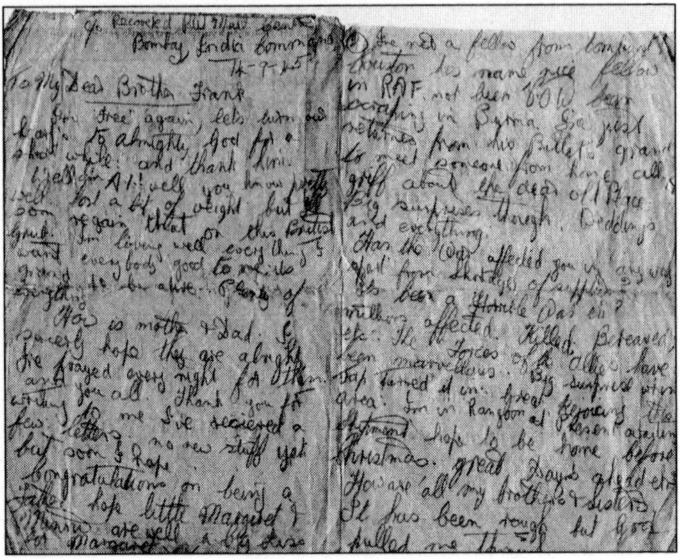

Bombay India [illegible]
14-9-45

To My Dear Brother Frank

I'm 'Free' again, lets [illegible] to Almighty God for a short while: and thank him. [illegible] A1! well you know pretty well. lost a bit of weight but soon regain that on this British grub. I'm living well everything & everybody good to me. its grand to be alive. Plenty of everything.

How is mother & Dad. I sincerely hope they are alright. I've prayed every night for them and you all. Thank you for writing to me I've recieved a few letters but soon I hope no new stuff yet

Congratulations on being a father hope little Margaret & [illegible] are well [illegible] for Margaret [illegible]

I've met a fellow from [illegible] his name [illegible] fellow in RAF. not been POW [illegible] escaping in Burma [illegible] just returned from his [illegible] grand to meet someone from home all griff about the dear old [illegible] big surprises though. Weddings and everything.

Has the War affected you in any way apart from shortage of supplies [illegible] its been a Horrible War eh? millions affected. Killed. Bereaved etc. The Forces of the Allies have been marvellous. Big surprise when Jap turned it in. Great rejoicing [illegible] area. I'm in Rangoon at present awaiting shipment hope to be home before Christmas. great days ahead eh?

How are all my brothers & sisters. It has been tough but God pulled me thro'

MY FIRST LETTER SENT HOME AFTER RELEASE.
WHILST AT RANGOON HOSPITAL

see page 210-211

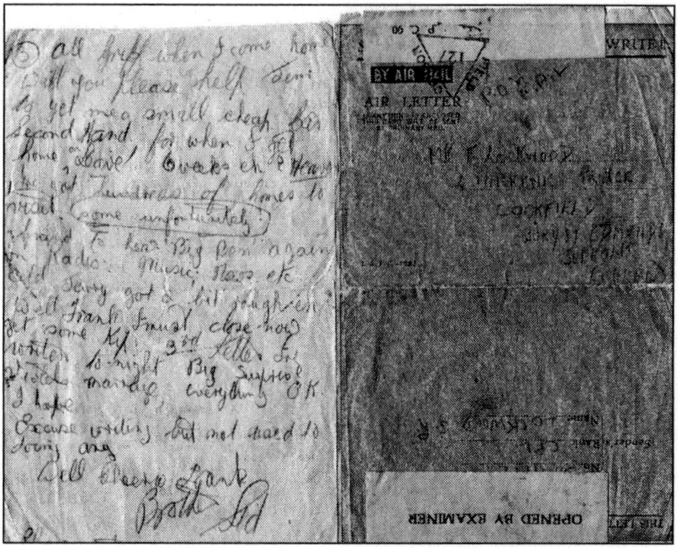

MY FIRST LETTER SENT HOME AFTER RELEASE. WHILST AT RANGOON HOSPITAL

(Note the dreadful scribble. I hadn't seen pen or paper for so long, let alone been able to write home.) *See page 210-211*

On day eleven, the supposed day of our departure from the hospital, it was the turn of George to do the postal run. Off he went. He hadn't been gone long when this corporal loudly called out my name. He must have been thinking he was talking to the fittest man in the land. He shouted at me, "Get up, Lockwood, get yourself ready and get out down to that boat, they are waiting for you downstairs to take you back to Blighty... come on, quick as you can." I quickly asked about my mate George, I must wait for him. "George Marritt is not well enough to go home, he's got to stay a further week," he retorted..."Come on, move it"... he was right blinking nasty to me, short and offhand. Why the aggression I don't know, he surely couldn't have been scared of me, not in my state, so why the need to shout? It still baffles me to this day. So off I went, not being allowed to wait to say goodbye to my dearest friend. As all these instructions were being bellowed at me, another orderly came around with a ration of beer and cigarettes for us all. He put two cans of beer on my bed and some cigarettes and the same with George's bed. So I thought, right... I've got to go, I've no choice, I've nothing to leave George a note with to explain my disappearance, so I quickly put my beer onto George's bed and whipped his fags. Off I went. Sadly after all this time together there were to be no final goodbyes.

My own opinion with hindsight all these years on, is that we should have never left Rangoon when we did. We should have been sent on to India or Australia for a recovery period of recuperation. We were not well enough to come away at this point.

However I made my way down the stairs and out of the hospital to an awaiting ambulance. I was driven right down to the dock's edge. As I clambered out of this ambulance, I saw this English-looking girl standing there. I said to her, "Hello my darling, where have you been all during this horrible war?" just like that... that was to be my only famous chat up line of the entire war I reckon, not having seen an English woman since leaving my dear Joyce on Bury St Edmunds station all those years ago.

She replied, "Just down the road from you all, I've been in Changhi gaol all the while." She went on to explain that she was a WAF and that they had been interned in the gaols but released about a month ahead of us. Having been dolled up in the meanwhile and given a new style uniform, the likes of which I hadn't seen back home, she told me she was sent to this aerodrome to help with the airlifting of the POWs to safety.

This was now the 26th September, they had been released a bit earlier, about 15th August.... but hey! ... I couldn't stop and talk to this female for long; this vast ship was waiting for me to board for Blighty. Remembering my hasty exit and lack of goodbyes with George from the Rangoon Hospital and so I went to make my way up the steps of the ship, when the girl said

"Wow... here is a half a crown for you to spend." Apparently that was her job, to issue each and every man with this money to help us out, so to speak. I should have kept that coin, it would have been worth a small fortune by now, wouldn't it!

CHAPTER TWENTY

1945

HOMEWARD BOUND

It was the 26th September 1945. Here was this mighty ship, the "Indrapoera" standing at the side of Rangoon Docks waiting for its weary cargo of frail ex-prisoners of war to go aboard and sail back to Blighty.

THE INDRAPOERA

I recall starting to alight those high metal steps, complete with my half crown tucked safely away for future use, when I realised I didn't have the strength to climb aboard this huge vessel. Why were they sending me home just yet? As much as I wanted to go back to see my family I felt almost unable to move or haul myself upwards. Those men that had ordered us to leave Rangoon hospital clearly had no conception whatsoever as to what we had just been through. As much as no news had filtered into camp from England, none whatsoever had been relayed to them about what went on inside those death camps.

However, enough of that. The Japs treated us far worse, that's for sure, but kindness and servility on behalf of some of those British officers at such a critical and moving time could have been improved upon.

This ship wasn't as large as the "Mount Vernon" we sailed out to Japan on, but it had beaten me, I was stuck. A paralysed feeling came over my legs and they just didn't have the wherewithal to drag my body higher up those steps. I thought I'm never going to get up there. I got half way up and then you turned the bend to climb up further. I couldn't go any further; I had no strength left in my body. Other boys were in the same predicament, none could really help the other. I stood there for a moment or two, got my breath back and then attempted the rest of the climb. Finally my weary body made it to the top. I felt I weighed six ton let alone six stone, then I grasped hold of the rails that go around the deck of the ship, looking down, seeing other men attempting what I had just done, I burst out crying. I just couldn't help myself, I sobbed and I sobbed... uncontrollably. I looked back down over the side of the ship and saw other men, my comrades, soldiers like me, all attempting the same heavy climb, many still on stretchers, and I could not help but weep aloud.

We had set off five years earlier to fight a war, to defend our country and its people. Here we were just freed from the most wicked of imprisonment imaginable, scarcely able to fend for ourselves and look after our own well-being. My heart felt totally broken and I was so overwhelmed by this whole experience, that the tears freely flowed for several minutes; my pent up emotions just simply poured out of me.

An orderly said, "Come on, mate, you can pack that up, you're on your way home now and I'll take you to where you have got to stay and sleep on the ship." So off I followed him, down the steps to the floor below, which was marked out with chalk as to where each man had to stay. So he showed me to my bed space and gave me two army biscuits and told me to stay put. I thought to myself… I'll stay here until you've gone out of the way ol` matey, then I'm out of here… I left my bits and pieces I had clung to, in the space allotted. As soon as the coast was clear I made my way back up on deck. My sadness was not eased back on deck. Still men were coming aboard, and still my crying continued. When another orderly came up to me and said that it was their duty and job to look after all of us men, and many men were suffering the same sad affliction as I was. Grown men overcome with grief beyond description. This orderly then ushered me further along and instructed me to sit down on the deck, whereupon he got me some hot tea and biscuits. He did his best to pacify me and many like me, and to settle us down for the onward journey, treatment the like of which many a man was receiving.

At 2.30 pm I was standing by the deck rails, watching all the events unfold and the "Indrapoera" sounded her loud hooter. A welcome sounding klaxon for a change, not the one sounding the start and end of a ten minute so-called tea break back at the jungle clearings, but a loud, deep throaty roar that warned of our huge vessel departing from the Harbour with its weary and emotional cargo of ex-POWs.

Free and away at last, then the ripple of a faint cheer went up. Gradually the cheers from us men became louder and louder, until we were shouting with sheer delight as we pulled away from the docks edge and out into the deep blue waters to sail back home. Thank God… words cannot tell how it felt to be free at last.

We had been sailing away for about two days when they brought letters around to us all. I was up on deck when I was handed some letters and it was there I read of the passing of my dear mother and father. It hit me really badly. That was the last thing I thought I was about to read. I felt numb, almost with disbelief at this sad news.

I was so looking forward to being reunited with them, holding them again, giving them both a kiss and telling them of my experiences. Now that was not to be. I felt robbed of my dearest possessions in life, unable to tell my parents of what had been happening to us all. Perhaps it was just as well they were to be spared this story for now.

Did they ever get my postcard? What about that message I had asked Cooper to relay to my family whilst I was waiting execution? Did they get that I wondered. They must have died thinking I was dead as they may not have heard from me in almost four years, it must have felt like an eternity to them, not hearing from me, and I was not the only son to be suffering from the war.

It was all too late, nothing could be done to stop these awful feelings of despair racing through my mind…I started crying again, I cannot tell you how I felt, words fail me even now.

Back then it was unbearable grief, a really deep sadness came over me. This news was simply terrible. I read the letters from my brother again and again, explaining the situation to me, but it changed nothing. The truth was dawning that they had both gone, so I naturally wrote home as soon as I could and below is the first letter I sent home after hearing such dreadful news.

I'm so grateful now that my brother Frank held on dearly to these letters.

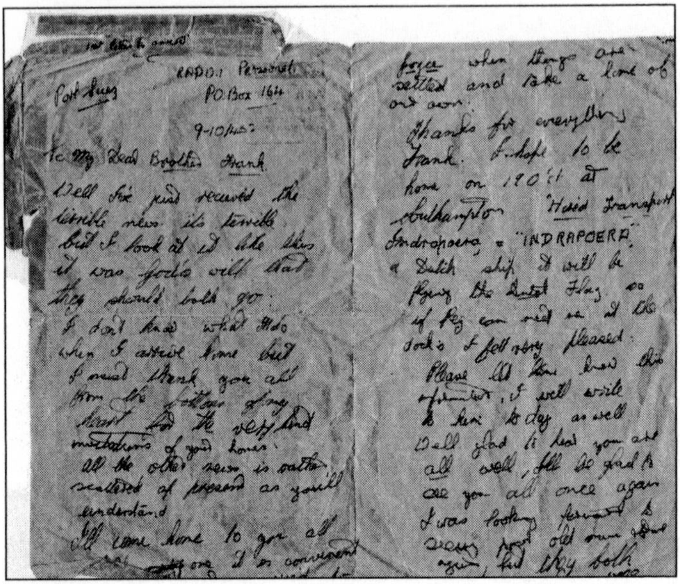

RAPO.I Personnel
Port Suez
P.O. Box 164

9-10-45

To My Dear Brother Frank
Well I've just received the
terrible news its terrible
but I look at it like this
it was God's will that
they should both go.
I don't know what I'll do
when I arrive home but
I must thank you all
from the bottom of my
heart for the very kind
invitations of your homes.
All the other news is rather
scattered at present as you'll
understand
I'll come home to you all
[illegible] one it is convenient

[illegible] when things are
settled and take a load of
our own.
Thanks for everything
Frank. I hope to be
home on 19 Oct at
Southampton "Hired Transport
Indrapoera" "INDRAPOERA"
a Dutch ship it will be
flying the Dutch Flag so
if they can meet me at the
docks I fell very pleased.
Please let [illegible] know this
information, I will write
to him to day as well
Well glad to hear you are
all well, I'll be glad to
see you all once again
I was looking forward to
seeing poor old mum & dad
again, but they both

LETTER SENT HOME FROM THE "INDRAPOERA" ON HEARING OF MY PARENTS DEATHS see page 212-213

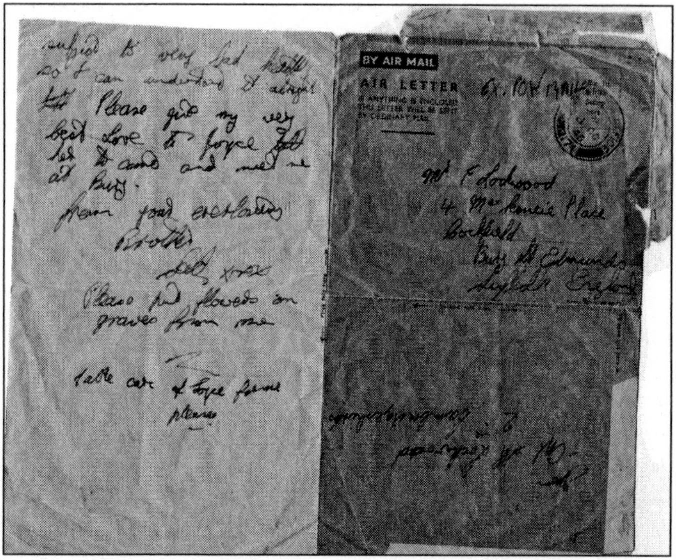

LETTER SENT HOME FROM THE "INDRAPOERA" ON HEARING OF MY PARENTS DEATHS see page 212-213

Other men were receiving the same sort of information from back home. We were encouraged to share our news and to talk to each other about the contents of our letters. Presumably a trouble shared is a trouble halved, but not in most cases, especially mine. News of parents, about the children, deaths in the family, one man said his wife had left him for another chap and so on and so on. All news was gradually filtering through after all these years of total silence. Some was met with joy but for the most part a lot of the news brought sorrow too. So now we had to come to terms with the real world again. Sad as that was, we had to deal with it all in our own way.

The orderlies had their hands full pacifying all of us chaps at the time, I can tell you, but they continually reassured us that they would help us through. I suppose it was now becoming apparent to us that our folks back home had mostly given up hope of ever seeing us alive again; possibly not having heard from us in four long years, naturally many people must have thought we had perished.

I guess too, that receipt on the "Indrapoera" of our post was held back on purpose for after a couple of days of sailing, to allow us to rest up a little perhaps from having seen similar reactions to previous letters, from POWs who had left the mainland on their earlier ships. The troops looking after us were becoming more accomplished and compassionate in how they dealt with their cargo of saddened men.

After about a week of sailing we called in at Colombo, Ceylon. We were to receive a gift from this country. Every ex-FEPOW was given a packet of tea to take home, real tea from Ceylon. This would have been worth quite a considerable penny or two back in those days.

Later we called in at Aden, as you come into the Suez Canal. We had some shore leave there; we were allowed to go ashore for a walk around. This is where we received our khaki uniform. So when we left Aden we had our full battle dress with us. I recall coming through the actual Suez Canal. It is narrow; you could almost touch the sides, so to speak, only one ship navigating through its waters at a time. There were places for ships to pull in to pass if necessary. It was lovely weather, I recall, and we were the only ship to be passing through at the time.

Once away from there and on towards Gibraltar, the weather worsened considerably. It turned really choppy at the Bay of Biscay. I remember wanting to use the toilet on board ship, which was across the ship's main top deck. The crew had already erected pig netting up of sorts around the decks rails for us to cling to if necessary, because the wind was so strong and the seas so rough, but more to save us skinny blokes from being washed overboard. You just could not walk up straight on top deck; the gale forced winds used to blow us backwards. Talk about a fag paper in the wind, that was us! I got hustled back right quickly, I can tell you!

So much for wanting to spend a penny. I grabbed hold of the fencing, struggled away to the toilet only to get washed in the face by the waves pounding up on the decks. Sea water splashing up and over everywhere. Still the camaraderie of sorts took place between the men. Some said if we all went to church that night, because it was so dark and rough we wouldn't see the lights of Gibraltar. Two or three of us said, "Don't you think so? You'll see."

We went to church on board the "Indrapoera" just the same as we did when and wherever we could. We came out of church, joined up with the men at the sides of the decks and still saw the welcoming lights from the Rock of Gibraltar. So that proved many of them wrong, didn't it! These were the first lights we had seen. That may seem a basic comment to make, but having lived without lights for so long, believe me it was a really heartwarming sight, glowing lights, warming up the blustery skies around us. Civilisation as we had left it years earlier, now became a reality and part of our homecoming as we sailed onwards to Southampton.

After lying off Southampton docks for a couple or so hours, the "Indrapoera", a Royal Rotterdam Lloyd vessel, eventually pulled alongside the quay at about 6am. It was raining really hard at the time. Some things don't change in years, do they! Before disembarkation could take place, we saw all these girls and women were standing at the quayside, ATS, WAFs etc, etc. All had come down to the harbour to meet their loved ones and were waiting for their husbands and boyfriends to walk safely ashore.... or so they thought!

I was looking down from the ships deck at the ladies, again many new style uniforms that we hadn't seen before, when one WAF called up to us on the top deck, asking if we had seen so and so? One bloke behind me blurted out, "Yes, he died up in Tarso." Tactless but to the point. Death had really become part of our everyday life, but to this lady it was her loved one, truly shocking news to be received in such an insensitive manner. Well, it was naturally all too much for her. She simply fainted on the quayside, landing amongst the gathering crowds, like a ton of bricks. I thought you blinking idiot, man, why didn't you just keep your mouth shut.

We eventually offloaded and left the "Indrapoera" to go about her duty on the high seas again, then we were chaperoned into a big dining hall. A huge man welcomed us to Southampton. We were given a meal and stayed one or two nights, how and where I stayed in the docklands I cannot recall. By this time I had written to my brother Frank to inform him of my planned homecoming time and place. Remarkably my letters were found at Frank's home some fifty or more years later. He had lovingly kept them all those years!

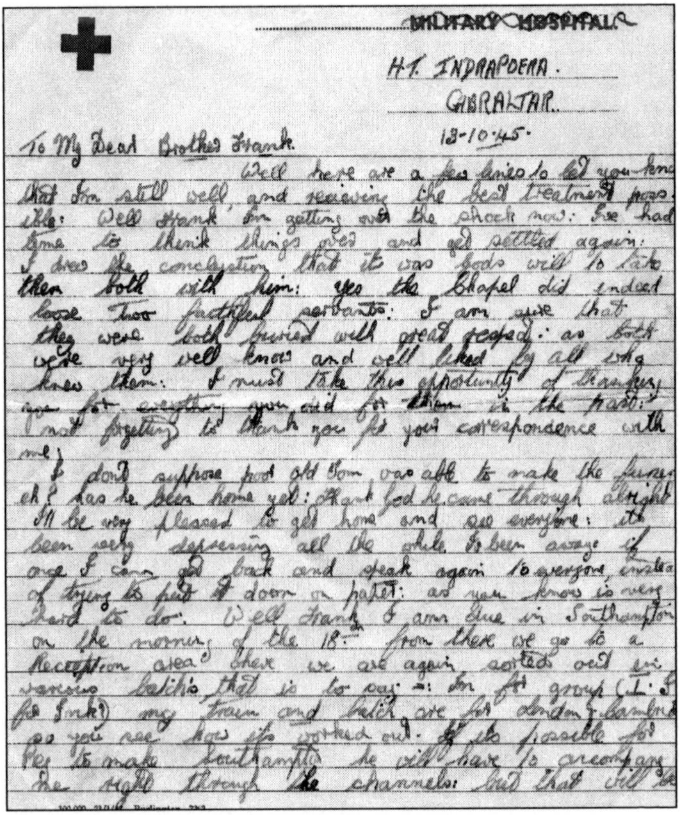

MILITARY HOSPITAL

H.T. INDRAPOERA.
GIBRALTAR.
13-10-45.

To My Dear Brother Frank.

Well here are a few lines to let you know that I'm still well, and receiving the best treatment possible: Well Frank I'm getting over the shock now: I've had time to think things over and get settled again: I drew the conclusion that it was Gods will to take them both with him: yes the Chapel did indeed loose two faithful servants: I am sure that they were both buried with great respect: as both were very well known and well liked by all who knew them: I must take this opportunity of thanking you for everything you did for them in the past: not forgetting to thank you for your correspondence with me;

I don't suppose poor old Tom was able to make the funeral eh? has he been home yet: thank God he came through alright I'll be very pleased to get home and see everyone: it's been very depressing all the while I've been away if once I can get back and speak again to everyone instead of trying to put it down on paper: as you know is very hard to do. Well Frank I am due in Southampton on the morning of the 18th from there we go to a Reception area there we are again sorted out in various batch's that is to say :- I'm for group (L: S for Lond?) my train and batch are for London & [illegible] as you see how it's worked out. If its possible for [illegible] to make Southampton he will have to accompany me right through the channels: but that will be

LAST LETTER SENT HOME FROM THE "INDRAPOERA"

See page 214-215

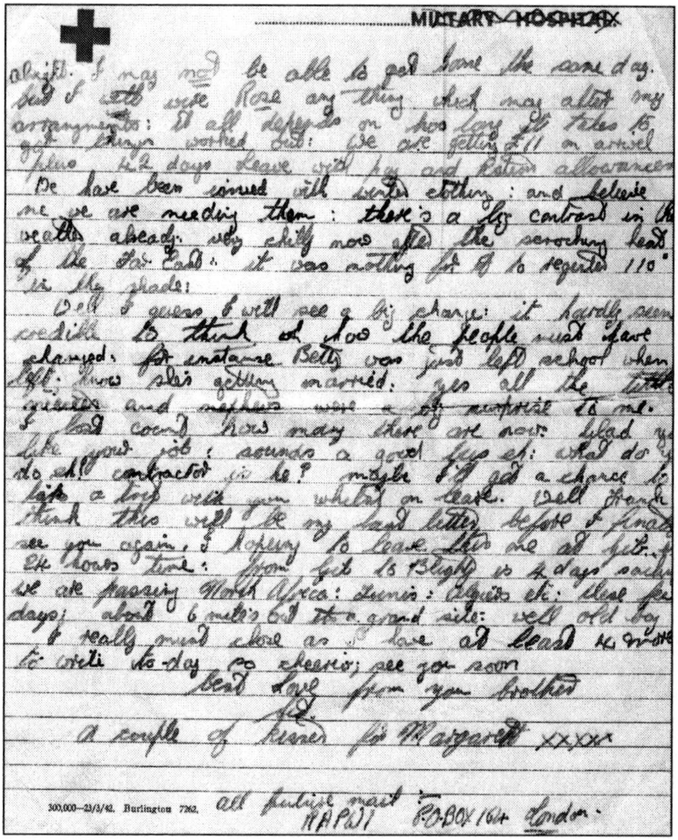
MILITARY HOSPITAL

alright. I may not be able to get home the same day.
but I will wire Rose any thing which may alter my
arrangements: it all depends on how long it takes to
get things worked out: we are getting £11 on arrival
plus 42 days leave with pay and Ration allowance
We have been issued with winter clothing: and believe
me we are needing them: there's a big contrast in the
weather already. very chilly now after the scorching heat
of the Far East: it was nothing for it to register 110°
in the shade:
Well I guess I will see a big change: it hardly seems
credible to think of how the people must have
changed: for instance Betty was just left school when
I left: now she's getting married: yes all the little
nieces and nephews were a big surprise to me.
I lost count how many there are now: glad you
like your job: sounds a good type eh: what do you
do all contractor is he? maybe I'll get a chance to
take a trip with you whilst on leave. Well Frank
think this will be my last letter before I finally
see you again, I hoping to leave this one at Gib. in
24 hours time: from Gib to Blighty is 4 days sailing
we are passing North Africa: Tunis: Algiers etc: these few
days; about 6 miles off the grand site: well old boy
I really must close as I have at least six more
to write to-day so cheerio; see you soon
Best Love from your brother
[illegible]
A couple of kisses for Margaret xxxx

300,000—23/3/42. Burlington 7262. all future mail: RAPWI P.O.BOX 164 London.

LAST LETTER SENT HOME FROM THE "INDRAPOERA"

(Note the Red Cross lined paper and this time I'm pleased to say my writing is somewhat improved.) *See page 214-215*

I did not know for sure who would come to meet me, if anyone would be able to in fact come from Cockfield to Southampton at all. A colonel had found out when the "Indrapoera" would be docking. In fact that information turned out to be a day late, but this information was contained in the letter above. On what was to be the last morning in Southampton, we were given a light breakfast. They still couldn't give us full rations as we were still unable to eat or stomach much food in any quantity.

It was in that breakfast hall that my name, rank and number was called out over the intercom. The blokes with me said, "Go on, Sid, that's you mate, off you go." So after saying many goodbyes, off I went down this path, when I met a really smartly uniformed fellow of a soldier coming towards me. I thought to myself I don't know who you are, I'm sure.

He spoke as we drew level and said, "Is that you, Joe?"

I stopped dead still in my tracks. Those words sounded sweet. It was the nickname given to me by my family.

I replied, "Yes, but who are you then?"

He quietly replied, "I'm your older brother Peg" (Edgar). It was four long years since we had seen each other, so naturally you can guess, it started me off crying yet again, tears of sheer relief to be reunited with my beloved brother again. He gently reassured me not to be so upset; he was there to take me back home. Peg had already in part had time to come to terms with our parents' death. It was 1943 my father died and May of 1945 when my mother passed away, so I missed seeing her by just six months. Now it was my time to come to terms with all the family news.

We went back to the padre's office, where we had a cup of tea together, and then the time came for us to collect our passes to leave the dock area. I knew the corporal had them on him in his desk, I had been watching from time to time and noticed that blokes were giving him money and cigarettes, gifts if you like, bribery of sorts I suppose. Then they would be handed over their passes and off they would go.

I asked if I could have my pass, giving him my details. He said, "No, you cannot have yours until tomorrow." I asked him why not. He gave the same insistent reply to which I told him my brother had travelled a long way to collect me and take me back home. He just stubbornly refused and replied it wouldn't be issued until tomorrow. With that I said, "Will a carton of cigarettes help you to release that pass today?" He soon of course agreed it would then be OK, no problems at all. So I handed over his "gift" of 200 cigarettes and duly got handed my pass to leave the premises.

He turned to my brother Peg and said, "Don't you dare take him out of the front gate, you'll have to squeeze out through the hedges at the back of the building." So off we finally went. That man must have made a small fortune out of us lot, it would have been small too, in comparison, half a crown here and there, the odd hand me outs... we didn't have a fortune to give, but this wise-eyed old blighter took what he could swindle out of us returning ex-POWs.

I kept up with brother Peg the best I could; he was still a fit soldier. He could see my plight and helped me along the way. We got onto the road and he said, "You stop here, ol` boy, I'll thumb us a lift to the station." With that he stood in the middle of the road and hailed down a jeep containing two Americans. Peg asked them it they would kindly drive us to Southampton railway station. The driver agreed, ordered us aboard his vehicle and they duly obliged with our request.

We waited on Southampton platform for the train to London and when it arrived it was absolutely packed to the rafters, crammed to capacity. There wasn't one seat to spare. Boys were sitting in the gangways, resting the best they could on their kit bags, lying on the floor, you name it. Every conceivable space was being used, but they had to squeeze even more of us on to this crowded train. We dossed down where we could find a few inches to spare and joined the throng for the homeward journey. I was feeling a little better by this time and eventually the train rolled into Paddington station, then we changed over to the Liverpool Street line for home, when Peg said, "Let's go and have a cup of tea and a bun." It was free and supplied by the WVS and very welcome it was too.

After our refreshments we made our way to the platform for Bury St Edmunds via Cambridge. The rail guard said, "You cannot go via Cambridge tonight, mate, you'll have to go via Ipswich and change at Stowmarket." So off we set, boarded the right train, still the same cramped conditions, nothing has really changed for rail travel over the decades, has it... except we were all travelling for free, somewhat different to prices paid out at today's tariff. It was to be Ipswich where the crowds aboard our train thinned a little and I was able to sit down for the first time in that day. It was a welcome seat and comfortable at that. After changing trains at Stowmarket we finally pulled into dear old Bury St Edmunds station just before daybreak at 2 am.

Peg and I got off the train and made to go down the stairs for the exit. Waiting on the edge of the platform were two Red Caps. Of course they laughed at Peg and insisted on seeing his pass, teasing him for being out at this time of the morning. He swiftly said, "Don't you worry about me, worry about him." Pointing at me. "He has just come out of a Japanese prison camp; he's hardly got the strength to stand up." Well, those two blokes swore and cursed because of what the Japs had done. Little did they know! So they asked what we had been instructed to do, so that could help us further along our journey. We went on to explain we were told an Army car would be waiting for us to take us home. It wasn't… so I was told to sit and wait up in the station and they would follow this up as nothing had arrived to take us home to Cockfield. They told me they would be gone half hour, so Peg went off with the two Red Caps hunting for our vehicle and driver at 2 am.

Eventually my brother and the two men returned only to say, "Sorry but no one will turn out for you at this time of morning mate, we'll have to summon you a taxi." Taxi… this time of morning, fat chance! But they succeeded, if I was willing to share with someone else. You bet of course I would share; I just wanted to get home now. So they helped me back down the stairs again. Away came this taxi; it had four Americans in it, plus two girls.

The taxi driver said to me "Hi, mate, you put your kit on the spare wheel at the front there, and you two get in the front with me.". He went on to explain that he had got to drop the two girls off at St Mary's Church, then take the four Americans on to Rougham. Passengers all safely dropped off as described, we made the moving journey out to Cockfield, and my long awaited homecoming was here. Peg and I were dropped off at the local post office. I asked what the damage was price-wise for the taxi, he replied, "£2 please." Where I found the money from beats me, goodness knows, somebody must have given me some money, I certainly don't recall how I came by it, but there it went, half crown and all I guess, taxi driver duly paid for his fare, and off he went.

With the passing of my mother and father since I had been gone, of course my parents' family home had been closed and items disposed of and shared out between my remaining brothers and sisters. My sister Rose had married Walter and was living right beside the post office. So this is where we made for, knocking on their door in the small hours of the morning. Walter put his head out of the bedroom window and said "Is that you, Sid?"

"Yes," I replied. Only for Walter to tell us both that we had got to go to sister Violet's up on the main green, where sister Rose was waiting for us to arrive.

Walter said, "You haven't got to come here, Sid. There is a bike in the shed if you want to use it." But brother Peg assured him we would walk. So walk about a mile to my other sister's house is what we had to do! We were both literally shattered by this time, even Peg was getting done for… and he was a fit-looking man.

My other sister Violet had also married whilst I had been away, to George Parker and was living up at Holly Cottage on Great Green. It was a lovely morning, still moonlit and at 4 am we knocked on the door of Holly Cottage… a banner with… WELCOME HOME SID… was above the door, put there by my two sisters. What a welcome, home at last with a family that cared. I cannot describe my immense relief.

We knocked loudly again to wake them all up. Rose answered the door and swiftly slammed it shut again in my face. She shouted through, "That's not Sid… that's not my brother out there."

Peg knocked again and said, "Come on Rose, it is Sid, I'm with him. It is him, open up please, let us in." The sight of me had scared her half stiff. Nothing had prepared Rose for the sight of this skinny, blackened, haggard and scared-looking younger brother. She remembered me as someone completely different from all those years earlier. I left as a fit and healthy, fresh-faced young man. Eventually they fully opened up the door and let us in. The reunion with them is still unforgettable, they all hugged me, we all burst out crying as we hugged each other, but never mind, I was home at last.

"Whatever have they done to you, boy?" asked Rose.

"They tried to kill us but never mind, I'm home, safe and alive that's all that matters now."

We settled down after our reunion and chatted. My younger sister Violet was very concerned about my state of health. Thinking she would be able to build me up overnight so to speak, she offered me a couple of hard boiled eggs. Needless to say I soon told her about the pails and pails of hard boiled eggs I had only just left behind. We laughed awhile, just a while and then out came the tea and biscuits. Much more palatable at the time, I have to say.

I'm not a greedy man even nowadays by any means, I do love and appreciate my food and have a real passion for apple pies, sausage rolls, Yorkshire puddings, stew and dumplings. I must say though, I do hate to see food wasted in any shape or form.

PHOTOGRAPH OF ME TAKEN SOME TIME AFTER MY RELEASE

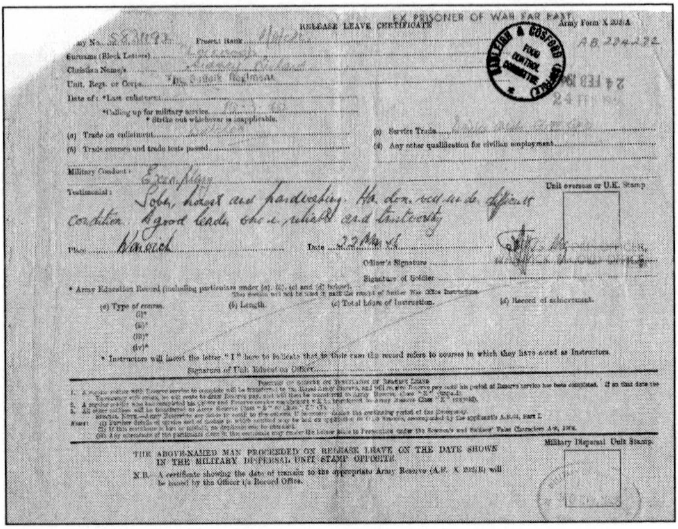
EX PRISONER OF WAR FAR EAST.

RELEASE LEAVE CERTIFICATE

Army Form X 202/A

AB 294232

Army No. 5831193 Present Rank [illegible]

Surname (Block Letters) [illegible]

Christian Name/s [illegible]

Unit, Regt. or Corps 4th Suffolk Regiment

Date of: *Last enlistment

*Calling up for military service [illegible]

* Strike out whichever is inapplicable.

(a) Trade on enlistment [illegible]

(b) Trade courses and trade tests passed

(c) Service Trade [illegible]

(d) Any other qualification for civilian employment

Military Conduct: Exemplary

Testimonial: [illegible]

Unit overseas or U.K. Stamp

Place Norwich Date [illegible]

Officer's Signature [illegible]

Signature of Soldier

* Army Education Record (including particulars under (a), (b), (c) and (d) below).

This section will not be used until the receipt of further War Office Instructions.

(a) Type of course. (b) Length. (c) Total hours of Instruction. (d) Record of achievement.

(i)*

(ii)*

(iii)*

(iv)*

* Instructors will insert the letter "I" here to indicate that in their case the record refers to courses in which they have acted as Instructors.

Signature of Unit Education Officer

[illegible]

Military Dispersal Unit Stamp

THE ABOVE-NAMED MAN PROCEEDED ON RELEASE LEAVE ON THE DATE SHOWN IN THE MILITARY DISPERSAL UNIT STAMP OPPOSITE.

N.B.—A certificate showing the date of transfer to the appropriate Army Reserve (A.F. X 202/B) will be issued by the Officer i/c Record Office.

DEMOB PAPERS

5—BURY FREE PRESS & POST, SEPTEMBER 11th, 1943

West Suffolk Forces News

(1) Cpl. T. R. Lockwood; (2) Pte. Arthur Bennett; (3) Cpl. Richard Howe.

Mr. and Mrs. George Bennett, of Church Road, Tostock, have received news that their eldest son, Pte. Arthur Bennett, 2nd Bn. Cambs. Regt., is a prisoner of war at Thailand Camp and is in excellent health and working for pay. Before the war he was employed by Mr. H. E. Mann, of Tostock.

Two post-cards have been received from Cpl. Richard Howe, 5th Bn. Suffolk Regt., missing since Singapore, son of Mr. and Mrs. B. Howe, 5, Bolton Street, Lavenham. Cpl. Howe says he is safe and well and working for pay. He was formerly employed by Mr. H. C. Steed, Lavenham.

News has been received that Cpl. S. R. Lockwood, 2nd Cambs. Regt., son of Mrs. and the late Mr. H. Lockwood, of White House, Cockfield, is a prisoner of war in Japanese hands, is well and getting good food. This is the first news received of him since the fall of Singapore. Before joining the Forces he was employed by Mrs. Golding, butcher, of Cockfield, and The Shambles, Bury St. Edmund's.

East Forces since 1941, and C
Joe Smith has been with
Mediterranean Fleet since 194

Mrs. Argent, of 23, St.
drew's Street, S., Bury St.
mund's, has been notified t
her husband, Petty Officer Jo
Harry Argent, is missing "a
operations." P.O. Argent is
only son of Mr. and Mrs. J.
gent, of the "King Willia
Long Brackland. He joined
Navy 9 years ago, when he
only 14½ years of age.

EAST ANGLIAN GIRLS

<u>A NEWSPAPER CUTTING FOUND AT MY BROTHER FRANK'S HOME NOTIFYING ALL THAT I HAD BEEN CAPTURED BY THE JAPANESE</u>

(You will note on reading that my Father had died without knowing of my plight.)

CHAPTER TWENTY-ONE

REBUILDING OUR LIVES

The colours of autumn were a warming sight to wake up to in the mornings. A cosy snug bed, sweet smelling bed linen and friendly chatter from downstairs. The familiar smells of breakfast wafting through the rooms.

I had only been home with my sisters for a day or so, when brother in law George was able to give Joyce a message from me that I was home safely. George incidentally worked with my Fiancée Joyce at a lovely big village home called Clipt Bushes owned by Miss Helen Ruffell. I had a couple of very early nights on my arrival home. Nine o'clock on the second morning home I made a telephone call to Clipt Bushes to speak with Miss Helen then of course she quickly put Joyce on the telephone to speak with me. I think she was so flabbergasted to hear my voice at long last, she found it just as hard to speak as I did. We agreed to meet that very same evening, but Joyce was reluctant to come into Violet's home straightaway. She wanted to meet up with me first, outside by the gate. She said, "I don't want to come to the door so please come out to the road to meet me first."

Right, so half past six it was to be that I would get to see my beloved Fiancée for the first time in over four long years. She had given up hope of ever seeing me alive long, long ago. Not hearing a word, she had presumed I was dead. It was dark and I was watching the clock tick away to six-thirty. Just as well I reckon by the time she arrived on her bike, we were so pleased to be back with each other. Naturally we had a few words outside together alone at last, then parked her bike up against the flint wall of the house and finally went back in to talk to the family again. Joyce had kept in regular contact with my parents and all my family throughout my years of captivity.

When we got inside in the light, Joyce was even more astounded at the very sight of me. "My word alive, what on earth has been going on, what ever have they done to you?" She was totally shocked. She couldn't believe her own eyes, seeing this stranger in front of her. A different-looking man from the youthful fresh-faced chappy she waved goodbye to all those years earlier. Obviously in the darkness my voice hadn't changed but all too clearly, now inside in the light my appearance to her was now somewhat startlingly different. Luckily she still loved me though, no matter what I looked like. The years had been kind to her. She was just as beautiful now as she was when I left for the Far East.

During the next few days I caught up with a lot of news, how Joyce and her family had coped, how her work had been going as a cook. She was working at Clipt Bushes which was right next to the airfield, so there were lots of stories to share about what she had seen happening there, with all the bomber activities. Catching up with friends and village life in general, who had served where and how had they all got on. Then I went to meet up again with Beatie and Rock Moss, my future in-laws and all of Joyce's brothers and sisters again. They had moved since I last saw them and were now living at Lamb's Lane in Lawshall. The size of some of those brothers still scares me today. They had certainly grown in the years I had been away. Remember then I only weighed in at just over the six stone mark and there were several of them, big ones at that, twelve siblings in all.

I attended chapel on my first Sunday home, this time complete with my brothers and sisters, despite feeling really groggy. I recall sitting two rows from the front much to the interest and of course delight of the congregation, whose prayers had sustained me and many like me from the villages around us, to get through those previous difficult years. Proof if proof were needed that God really does answer our prayers. So much so, that a lovely lady and life time friend as it turned out, Mrs Adeline Hubbard, turned up at sister Violet's home at around 2.30 pm this particular Sunday with a whole chicken for me. Gosh, I must have looked like I needed a jolly good meal. I was naturally polite and very grateful to her for this generous gift, knowing that it would serve the family very well indeed, but as for me, well I just picked at this and that for a long while, totally unable to digest a full meal of any kind as yet.

The following days my sister Violet's little baby boy was in fact too much for me to bear. That sounds a sad statement to make after being away from family life for so long; you would have really thought that I would have loved the company, whatever the age group. The truth of the matter was I couldn't put up with the noise and the scampering around of the youngster, so my sister Rose said she thought I would be able to rest better if I went down to their cottage by the post office instead with her and Walter.

So I rested up with Rose, Walter and their son, who was an older lad and quieter to be around with; his sister Betty was working away somewhere, I don't recall where.

I'd been home about a fortnight, I reckon, when I became very ill indeed. I was so ill they didn't know what to do with me at the time. They had an old-fashioned stove in their room and I sat right in the fireplace itself, I wasn't worried about burning myself, I just needed to get warmed through, nestling up against it covered in a blanket because I was so cold, chilled to the bone.

This was in the times when the local tradesman used to knock at the door and walk straight into your home, lovely trusting days, different to today in many ways. Mr George White our local grocer arrived with the weekly shopping and to collect the next week's order, when he asked about me and how I was. Rose said, "Go straight through, George, he's by the fire."

George took one look at me and I recall his words vividly. "You're not going to die are you Sid?"

I soon replied, "No not likely, not now but I do need help. Can you please call a doctor for me?" So he took Rose to the local telephone box and made the all-important call, only to return stating the doctor didn't know what to do with tropical illness so to call an ambulance instead. This they did and called the Army ambulance service out to collect me. The ambulance arrived and I decided I was well enough to travel in the front with the two medical men.

We arrived at the old Bury hospital wards, which had covered walkways, so once again I decided to walk up to the hospital entrance. Only to be greeted by Nurse Sister Dosser who chopped into those two Army men, ripping them apart for allowing me to even walk. Pity she wasn't back in Thailand to deal with the rather loud RSM; she would for sure have melted his hard heart. I said to her, "Well, excuse me, please don't have a go at them, I thought I could manage this for myself." I was soon told I had a temperature of 104 and quickly hustled and ushered into the ward and into the first bed inside the door. I was in fact the first patient in there on my own but clearly they were waiting for me and many more to follow like me; as it would soon transpire their predictions were correct.

I was there for three days and totally confounded them as to how they would be able to deal with my illness, when someone said that they should call a German doctor who was interned at a local doctor's house in town, as he specialised in tropical medicines. He was summoned and arrived within the hour. He soon diagnosed my condition as malaria and I recall him saying, "This is it, in its worst form ever possible. This man will drift in and out of consciousness over the next few days." He was right, my memory played tricks with me for several days. I just didn't know where I was. He went on to instruct them that the only chance I had was to be administered quinine, which miraculously they located and found in a Colchester hospital, not having any at Bury St Edmunds. They had it quickly collected and brought over and given to me.

I was there in hospital for about one month. The early days I was not allowed visitors. I guess they didn't expect me to pull through that particular bout of malaria. But I did get well and stronger again. After Thailand nothing could ever be that bad in life again, no matter what!

I was eventually strong enough to return to my sister's. Brother Jim called at Rose's one morning to tell me that his boss wanted to see me, he didn't explain why, just to say to go down that evening to see him and his wife. So off I duly trundled, gingerly on my bike in the dark again, at about 6.30 pm and made my way to Water Lane Haulage Depot in Little Whelnetham, just outside of our town and owned by the late Mr and Mrs Ted Sharpe. On arrival I was cordially invited in, I didn't know this family at the time, only to be offered tea and cakes. My word, how I must have looked to everyone, all these Ladies wanting to feed me up with their home baking, I was beginning to relish the attention, not to mention the food.

Mr Sharpe discussed matters with me and left me by saying, "Do take a couple of months rest to recuperate and them come back and join me as a lorry driver?" This I did. He had promised that I could just chauffeur the lorry and he would send a man with me to do all the work. I reported for work some weeks later and there stood this Dodge lorry with a hood over the buck and he said to me that I was to take this lorry to the prison camp at Hardwick to take German prisoners to their day's work. I said, "I cannot do that, they'll make mincemeat of me."

He said, "You can."

To which I replied, "I cannot go with German prisoners of war" but he was an insistent employer and said I was to go. So I took the lorry to Bury St Edmunds and they loaded me up with about 30 German prisoners and one of their superiors got in the front with me. I thought good gracious they'll eat me alive! I'm happy to say they didn't. I dropped them off at their respective farms where they were to carry out their day's labour. I dropped the last men off at about 11 am and had to remain there with the lorry on that farm until about 3.30 pm and then start picking them all up again for the return journey to their prison camps.

This routine carried on for several weeks, until the Germans were sent back home. To think that it was a German doctor's visit and knowledge of tropical medicines that had helped me out in such a way back in the early days at West Suffolk Hospital. What irony this was for my first job!

After this I was placed on general haulage duties, visiting farms to collect bags of grain. The lorries were fitted with hydraulic sack lifts and Mr Sharpe kept his word and sent a man with me to do the heavy work, by the name of Billy Frost; he was a big strong boy. All I did was to drive from A to B. Billy was a true comrade in every sense of the word. He loaded the lorry with the sacks of barley and I drove to the maltings and back to the farms. Time passed working in this manner and it was thought after a period of time that I would now at least be able to try to manage on my own. So what happed was Mr Sharpe sent two lorries on the same job, Billy and myself. Do you know Billy would load his lorry and then turn round and say to me, "Come off there, I'll do that, you cannot manage yet, Sid, I'll load yours as well." What utter strength this man had, I felt so humble and feeble at not being able to lift these heavy sacks across my back, not yet anyway. You see barley came in sixteen stone sacks, wheat in eighteen stone sacks and clover weighed in at 22 stone, all of which took some lifting, especially by a skinny little bloke like me. So I was truly indebted to Billy as he enabled me to keep my job and to earn a living for my family. Without that support who knows?

Eventually my health changed but not necessarily for the better, I was in and out of hospital again, meeting up with Sister Dosser again and again. Both her and Dr Cochran knew what kind of state I was in. The doctor told me to eat a little piece of chocolate as often as I could, and do you know I haven't stopped eating chocolate yet... I love it...

As my strength returned and my health improved I continued with the lorry driving and I was privileged to travel the length and breadth of the country, even into Scotland and Wales. I certainly got to know my way about, that's for sure. I worked for Mr Sharpe for twenty-six years until he had to retire and eventually close his business down. Memorable and enjoyable years spent with a remarkable man and his family.

LORRIES WERE MY WORKING LIFE

I married Joyce during that time. On April 20th 1946 we were married at Lawshall Church. The infamous Canon Wintle officiated at our ceremony, he being well known around the country for his barrel organs, one of which still stands in York museum today. We went on to celebrate our union with our two large families. Rationing was still on so Joyce and her sisters carried out most of the cooking and baking preparation for the wedding day. Her sister Flo made our wedding cake. Joyce went down with laryngitis before the actually big day but thankfully she managed to croak "I do"... and all went according to plan, except for the heat of the beautiful day melting our wedding cake and toppling the first top tier, on our arrival at the village hall.

OUR WEDDING DAY 1946

Our one and only baby arrived in June of 1947 and we raised Barbara at Holly Bush Cottage on the edge of Cockfield Green, my sister Violet's first home and now to be our first home, which the Golding family kindly allowed us to live in for a very low rent, about 3s 6d per week as I recall. A far cry from the average rent or mortgage of today. Eventually we were awarded a council house and lived at the Green until 1994. We spent many happy years there and tended a very well kept garden. You could hear and see the spade in the garden clinking away in the moonlight many a night, to provide food for the kitchen table.

Before our final house move to Bury town, I certainly was not a well paid man. Earlier, if I cleared £10 a week I had managed a good week. Clocking up long hours in the bargain, many is the time that Joyce would be waiting for the bus on the edge of the green to go to town, to get us this or that, and would be waiting patiently for me to arrive home Saturday lunch time on my bike, complete with my desperately awaited wage packet to enable her to get on the once weekly bus, to go into town and get the necessary bits and bobs for the family, but they were happy days. We often had Beatie and some of her family over on a Sunday; it was a regular occurrence to all sit down to Sunday lunch together.

I then went on to join other lorry firms, Waspe of Cockfield pipe carrying, Hunt of Bradfield carrying livestock, pigs, cows, sheep even great big horses, the likes of which I started my working days with Hodge at Cockfield working on the land. Then onto Wilson's back to carrying grain. I finished my days working for Bells of Colchester as they bought out Wilson's. So I got to drive many different lorries, all of which I have to say you would have been proud to sit in, as they were kept immaculately clean and tidy. I could tell you a whole lot more stories about my escapades driving but enough for now, I have included a couple of special photographs of me working with the beloved lorries. Still today I read all I can about these vehicles and take regular monthly magazines just to keep abreast of all the changes and there are some mighty machines on the road today. I take great pleasure when we have a trip out with my daughter in seeing how many lorry haulage firms I know of and can recall.

It was well into our seventies and due to my wife becoming ill with cancer, we moved into Bury St Edmunds. We now live with our daughter on the edge of the town, having made many dear friends and having spent 75 memorable years in my beloved village of Cockfield.

Joyce was certainly a good cook, a skill that she put to effective use time and time again in helping our little congregational chapel at Cockfield. Cooking batches of cakes and buns ready for every Good Friday for a special tea that we all provided for over one hundred people to partake in. I should add at this point that I eventually took over the running of this chapel and we successfully carried on with our two services on Sundays for many years, until the numbers were so depleted that we had to hand over the running of this chapel to another denomination. Due to age and my wife's health it was timely to let someone else take the reins and lead in God's house. After that period in time, we moved into Bury to live with our daughter who now takes good care of the both of us. Now I too can make a tasty dumpling for the stew.

CLOSE TO RETIREMENT DAYS AND STILL ENJOYING THE DRIVING EXPERIENCE

Not long after retirement I suffered a major operation for duodenal ulcer which wasn't without its complications, the scars and hernias still present today, but nonetheless I made a good recovery.

I should add at this point that it was whilst clearing my late brother Frank's home in the 1980s after his death, that I came across the letters I have shared with your earlier. You can imagine my surprise and sheer delight at finding them. To say I shed a tear when I read them is an understatement. That was not to be the only surprise I unearthed from his home. There sat an aspidistra stand proudly in the corner behind his bed. I said to my daughter, "If that's not some of my handiwork I'll eat my hat." So together we quickly turned the table upside down only to find my name scribbled in pencil underneath. It was a table that I had made when I was 11 years of age. I used to go to Lavenham to be taught by a local carpenter, along with Harold Tricker (Tucker) and Jim Long, to name but two from my village school. Off we used to go on the local village bus, on a Wednesday morning once a week for a number of weeks. I am proud of that table which now stands in my daughter's house, just as proud as I was when I took it home to my mum and dad all those years earlier. Here it now stood in front of me in brother Frank's home. I hadn't even seen it in all those years of visiting him, it being tucked away in my brother's bedroom. It had survived untouched almost, so I did get something from my parents' home to treasure after all.

After many years of trying to trace George Marritt, my niece finally tracked him down in York for me. After initial correspondence, we soon went about sorting out a reunion and here is the photograph of the two of us, face to face, smiling at each other again after some forty-seven or more years. It was a wonderful moment, neither having clapped eyes on each other since I departed so swiftly from Rangoon Hospital in 1945, whilst he was out collecting the post. Remember I was called to join the "Indrapoera" to go home, and my dumping the cans of beer on his bed and whipping his cigarettes, then swiftly having to clear off. Now at last we were able to catch up and explain what happened then, along too with all the news of the missing years, and being able to meet up with his lovely wife Jessie. We have thankfully been in touch ever since and enjoy many a chat over the telephone as long distance makes it impossible for us to get together nowadays.

THE REUNION WITH GEORGE MARRITT

Joyce and I celebrated our 50th wedding anniversary in 1996. George and Jessie were well enough to spend the weekend with us all. It was a surprise party for about 120 guests, mostly family but also many true friends from Cockfield and around. As you see between the 22 initial offspring of which we were the siblings, the Lockwoods and the Mosses have many little ones of their own. Enjoying a Country and Western musical evening, we all celebrated in true style, a very memorable and enjoyable time and thankfully Joyce had recovered from her operation sufficiently enough to enjoy every moment of our special day.

SIDNEY & JOYCE GOLDEN WEDDING
APRIL 20th 1996

I spend happy hours tending our little garden in Bury and have a constant companion by my side answering to the name of Sooty. That cat would talk if he could. Well, I actually think he does! Joyce is able to get out and about sometimes with the aid of her wheelchair and here is a picture of the two of us enjoying the flowers at our local Abbey Gardens.

We have to take life in the slower lane now but both feel so fortunate to be reasonably well and both halfway through our eighties. So we have much to thank God for on a daily basis.

SOOTY OUR CAT

JOYCE AND ME IN THE ABBEY GARDENS

Before I end my story I will leave you with a picture of some of my dear friends, all ex-POWs, just before we were to be presented to her Majesty Queen Elizabeth II and Prince Philip as they travelled through Bury St Edmunds Abbey Gardens.

Here I must leave my journey as a prisoner of war through Thailand and of my life story. I trust you have found it of interest and in the process have learnt something of the hardship endured by the many prisoners of war like myself, held captive under the Japanese Imperial Army. In my case for over three and a half years from early 1942 to late 1945.

SOME TRUE COMRADES AND DEAR FRIENDS

AND FINALLY

All of our misfortune was overshadowed by an enormous feat of engineering by the Japanese Imperial Army and the might of its many soldiers. Visitors from across the world now travel to Thailand, I'm sure, for its beauty and to see that wonderful land, but also to see for themselves the infamous railway built by slave labourers, those held prisoner from many other nations including our own.

I just hope and pray that visitors don't just admire the breathtaking scenery and the railway itself. The many bridges, the engines that remain, the track that is left and the museums, without pausing to reflect upon the pain and suffering that happened during its creation. I'm sure everyone must be moved in their own particular way at the sights and knowledge of the history surrounding this nation. Many visitors I'm sure are also trying to retrace their parents' life all those years ago.

Much of the line and the camp areas must have eroded with time or have been lost to the intense undergrowth and vegetation of today. Doubtless much of the area has been built upon to serve this growing nation. I hope also that not just the visitors to Thailand, but that the many readers of books, those who watch the associated films to that region, those who listen to the many debates and documentaries, have been in some way able to grasp the raw reality of the personal sacrifices, the many needless deaths, the true horror, evil starvation, all coupled with the serious illnesses that ensued as a direct result of captivity under such awful conditions.

Perhaps by passing in and through the military cemeteries, it sobers the minds of the onlookers and causes them to realise its not just neat rows of stone crosses, not just one name they may be wanting to trace, but truly believe, that beneath it all lays the memory of a hard-working lost soul. Many a lost loved one and many a lost friend, especially for us remaining ex-prisoners of war who served alongside those thousands of departed soldiers of war.

It was a hugely complicated and enormous logistical task, a railway line covering hundreds of miles, crossing rivers, skirting around hills and mountainsides, passing many little villages and their inhabitants, crossing over from one country to another. Tearing into virgin jungle, ripping their countries apart to build this famous railway line from Ban Pong to Rangoon. All those sleepers laid during those years of captivity represented a life lost in its creation.

It is clear that errors were made, on both sides I'm sure, and with hindsight this bloodshed should and could have been avoided, but that is the sad price of any war, even then and indeed now.

I can only conclude by saying I was truly lucky to survive along with my friends that came home with me. Since I have been home I have been blessed with a lovely wife to share my life with and a daughter who has helped us both enormously, and I thank God for all those blessings every single day.

I do thank my daughter for her tremendous support in helping me to write my story. Without her I could not have told you about my time as a prisoner of war. Barbara and I have spent many hours piecing this together. What seems like an unbelievable story but nevertheless it is a true one.

I would say to my friends, those from the reunion clubs, those who walked with us on the marches, we have all been blessed to be able to return from those camps of hell, many names too numerous to mention for fear of missing an important name out. But, thank you one and all, for your continued support over the years, and for the kind deeds that so many of you have willingly and freely done. Including the yearly reunion get-together, monthly club meetings, dinners and teas and long may it all continue.

We all know that we will never forget those comrades we left behind, and leave them to rest in God's care until we meet and see them all again. We can draw strength from the added blessings of so many life-long friends that without the happenings of war, and of us being held prisoners together, would never have come to pass. Having such friends it's true to say, that despite everything we endured, I would not have wanted to miss out on enjoying their friendship for all the world.

I would like to add my personal thanks to those who have kindly allowed me to use their photographs to help portray my story.

LETTER ONE

c/o Recovered P.W. Mail Centre Command,
Bombay,
India.

14.09.45

To My Dear Brother Frank,

I'm "free again". Let's turn our hearts to Almighty God for a short while and thank him.

Well, I'm A1, Well you know pretty well, lost a bit of weight but I'll soon regain that on this British grub. I'm living well, everything I want, everybody good to me; it's grand to be alive. Plenty of everything.

How is Mother and Dad? I sincerely hope they are all right, I've prayed every night for them, and you all. Thank you for writing to me. I've received a few letters, no new stuff yet but soon I hope.

Congratulations on being a Father, hope little Margaret and Minnie are well, a big kiss for Margaret. X.

I've met a fellow from Combust, Couston his name, nice fellow in R.A.F. not been POW been scraping in Burma. I've just returned from his billets, grand to meet someone from home. All griff about the dear old place. Big surprises though, Weddings, and everything.

Has the war affected you in any way, apart from shortages of supplies?

It's been a Horrible war eh? Millions affected. Killed, Bereaved, etc.

The Forces of the Allies have been marvellous. Big surprise when Jap "turned it in". Great rejoicing this area.

I'm in Rangoon at present awaiting shipment; hope to be home before Christmas. Great days ahead eh!

How are all my Brothers and Sisters? It has been rough but God pulled me through.

All griff when I come home. Will you please help Jim to get me a small cheap car. Second hand, for when I get home on leave, 6 weeks eh? and <u>*Heaven.*</u> *I've got hundreds of homes to visit, (some unfortunately!)*

Grand to hear "Big Ben" again on Radio. Music, News, etc.

Old Jerry got a bit rough, eh?

Well Frank I must close now get some kip, 3rd letter I've written tonight. Big surprise Violet's marriage, everything O.K. I hope.

Excuse writing but not used to doing any

Well cheerio Frank
Brother Sid

Please write.

LETTER TWO

R.A.P.W.I. Personnel
P.O. Box 164
Port Suez

09.10.45.

To My Dear Brother Frank

Well I've just received the terrible news, it's terrible, but I look at it like this, it was God's will that they should both go.

I don't know what I'll do when I arrive home, but I must thank you all from the bottom of my heart for the very kind invitations of your homes

All the others news is rather scattered at present as you'll understand.

I'll come home to you all to which one it is convenient, I shall get married to Joyce when things are settled and take a home of our own.

Thanks for everything Frank. I hope to be home on 19th Oct. at Southampton "hired transport Indrapoera = INDRAPOERA" a Dutch ship, it will be flying the Dutch flag, so if Peg can meet me at the docks I'll feel very pleased.

Please let him know this information, I will write to him today as well.

Well glad to hear you are all well, I'll be glad to see you all once again. I was looking forward to seeing poor old Mum and Dad again, but they both were subject to very bad health, so I can understand it all right.

Please give my very best love to Joyce and tell her to come and meet me at Bury.

From your ever loving Brother
Sid x x

Please put flowers on graves from me

Take care of Joyce for me please

LETTER THREE

H.T. INDRAPOERA
GIBRALTAR
13.10.45

To My Dear Brother Frank

Well here are a few lines to let you know that I'm still well, and receiving the best treatment possible. Well Frank I'm getting over the shock now. I've had time to think things over and get settled again.

I drew the conclusion that it was God's will to take them both with him.

Yes the Chapel did indeed lose two faithful servants. I am sure that they were both buried with great respect, as both were very well known and well liked by all who knew them.

I must take this opportunity of thanking you for everything you did for them in the past, not forgetting to thank you for your correspondence with me.

I don't suppose poor old Tom was able to make the funeral eh? Has he been home yet. Thank God he came through all right.

I'll be very pleased to get home and see everyone, it's been very depressing all the while I've been away, if once I can get back and speak again to everyone, instead of trying to put it down on paper, as you know is very hard to do.

Well Frank I am due in Southampton on the morning of the 18th from there we go to a Reception area, where we are again sorted out in various batches that is to say, I'm for the group (I, for Ink). My train and batch are for London and Cambridge, so you see how it's worked out. If it's possible for Peg to make Southampton he will have to accompany me right through the channels, but that will be all right. I may not be able to get home that same day, but I will wire Rose anything which may alter my arrangements. It all depends on how long it takes to get things worked out. We are getting £11 on arrival, plus 42 days leave with pay and Ration allowances.

We have been issued with winter clothing and believe me we are needing them, there is a big contract in the weather already, very chilly now after the scorching heat of the Far East, it was nothing far off to register 110 degrees in the shade.

Well I guess I will see a big change, it hardly seems credible to think how the people must have changed, for instance Betty was just left school when I left, now she is getting married, yes all the little nieces and nephews were a big surprise to me. I lost count how many there are now.

Glad you like your job, sounds a good bus eh? What do you do eh? Contractor is he? Maybe I'll get a chance to take a trip with you whilst on leave

Well Frank I think this will be my last letter before I finally see you again. I'm hoping to leave this one at Gib. In 24 hours time.

From Gib to Blighty is 4 days sailing, we are passing North Africa, Tunis, Algiers etc. These few days about 6 miles but it's a grand sight.

Well old boy I really must close as I have at least 4 more to write today, so cheerio, see you soon

Best Love from your Brother Sid
A couple of kisses for Margaret x x x x x

All future mail: - R.A.P.W.I
P.O. Box 164
London

THE DAY THOU GAVEST, LORD, IS ENDED

This is Dad's favourite of all hymns

It was sung in the prison camps in their makeshift church areas for as long as it was permitted, until the order was given for church worship to be abandoned and totally forbidden by the Japanese.

The last time this hymn was sung on camp was near to the Three Pagoda Pass, about six months before the ending of captivity.

About 100 or so men remained in that particular camp and about twelve men stood in the doorway of their hut and sang this hymn through from memory, accompanied by one POW who had miraculously still held onto his old piano accordion.

Imagine their thoughts for just one moment more, as you ponder the verses of this well known hymn:

The day Thou gavest, Lord, is ended
The darkness falls at Thy behest
To Thee our morning hymns ascended
Thy praise shall sanctify our rest

We thank Thee that Thy Church unsleeping
While earth rolls onwards into light
Through all the world her watch is keeping
And rests not now by day or night

As o'er each continent and island
The dawn leads on another day
The voice of prayer is never silent
Nor dies the strain of praise away

The sun that bids us rest is waking
Our brethren 'neath the western sky
And hour by hour fresh lips are making
Thy wondrous doings heard on high

So be it Lord, Thy throne shall never
Like earth's proud empires, pass away
Thy kingdom stands and grows for ever
Til all Thy creatures own Thy sway